Reviews of: *How I Died*

"This is one of the most wonderful spiritual books I've ever had the privilege of reading. It is full of touching human stories, but told from a soul rather than a human perspective. Our loss of basic spiritual understanding in the modern Western world has allowed death to become a great taboo, but this book should go a very long way in helping people to let go of their fear, not only about their own death but also that of their loved ones."
* Ian Lawton, author of *Rational Spirituality*

This wonderfully optimistic book by Jenkins and Winninger is based on authentic communications with those who have gone beyond. As one who has known Peter for many years, I can attest to the integrity of his insights and testimonies. Doubts and misgivings about life after death can be set aside with the gift of this special book.   * Dr. Austin Ritterspach, Ph.D. Religious Studies, Indiana University Purdue University Indianapolis.

"Death is the great unknown. The fear of it is buried deep within our subconscious and restricts our evolution. This book demystifies the subject and sets us free. It is a fascinating and illuminating read. The Masters chose an interesting and diverse selection of stories, presenting them with their customary lucidity."   * Jane Ritson, Psychological and Spiritual Astrologer

"Dying can be such a beautiful experience. The book will definitely help many people heal their fear of dying and the loss of their loved ones. Thank you for such a great book."
* Toh Lee Sin, Director Love & Light Festival, Singapore

"This is an amazingly good read and full of wonderfully interesting accounts of people's death. What I liked most are the narratives of people who at death became discarnates: ghosts and spirit attachments. This area is just coming to humanity's awareness and this book will greatly help."
* Andy Tomlinson, Director, the Past Life Regression Academy.

i

How I Died (and what I did next)

How we experience physical death

How I Died
(and what I did next)

Accounts Given by Souls on the Other Side

Compiled by
Peter Watson Jenkins

Channeled by
Toni Ann Winninger

~ Celestial Voices, Inc. ~

Acknowledgements

Our thanks are due to
Twenty-five souls who took part
The Ascended Masters for the idea
and for facilitating the book's progress
to our human assistants
Sonia Ness and Betty Hernandez
for help with the manuscript.
and to Robin Wade for his
hard work and support.

Contents

Celestial Voices, Inc.

The Masters of the Spirit World
are supported on planet Earth
by our small publishing house.
We run the Masters' weblog,
a Facebook page and publish
books and pamphlets on
the theme of reincarnation,
the journey of the soul.
*
www.CelestialVoicesInc.com

Introduction

This collection of studies, *How I Died (and what I did next)*, comprises personal recollections by twenty-five souls of their most recent physical death and subsequent journey Home to the dimension of unconditional love. Each of the souls have been selected by our guides, the Masters of the Spirit World, to contribute to this book. All of them understood the purpose of the book and, needed no prompting to tell their personal stories in their own way.

We had discussed this idea with the Masters, with whom we have been privileged to write several books. They agreed that Peter Watson Jenkins conduct the interviews and Toni Ann Winninger, who is a clear channel, translate the vibrational reports given by their chosen subjects. These souls recalled lives in many parts of the world, mostly in the twentieth century. In their transition from human to spirit life, they had experienced a variety of circumstances ranging from a quiet death in old age to sudden or violent terminations of their physical existence.

In assembling the stories, there was little need for our input in selecting the individual souls who actually took part in the project. We did request that the Masters' selection would give a world perspective, and that the circumstances of each death should be clearly different. As things turned out we found ourselves in a position of total overload, with masses of souls reportedly volunteering to tell their story. There are so many variations on the theme of death, and so many places and times from which accounts may be taken—yet we had only one small book in which to put a handful of them. We cannot claim to have done more by publishing these stories than to roughly sketch the picture of transition from this life and, with varying detail, give a little glimpse of what happens to ordinary people when they "cross over."

The purpose of this book should be quite plain. Our hope is to share this experience so that you may become attuned to the reality of transition from this physical world to the spirit realm back Home, and lose the very human— but entirely erroneous—fear of being snuffed out forever by Death, the grim reaper, in the final act of physical life. So far as we know, before this book was written nobody had solicited help from the Other Side so that a group of souls, who had made the journey themselves, might relate in detail the actual events of their death and subsequent transition.

In presenting for your consideration these personal histories told by souls living on the Other Side, we are aware that those of a nervous disposition may instinctively shy away from some of the most heart-rending stories, but we are convinced that it is truly healthy for everyone to have a clear vision of what really happens at death. Several of these accounts have distressful graphic moments in them—so please be very careful how you share them with children. Those containing the most graphic descriptions have been noted as such under their respective chapter headings.

The Masters are offering you here an opportunity to be stimulated and enriched by contact with these beautiful souls. We purposely did not ask for famous or influential people to be our subjects, as we did in our previous books of interviews. All souls are equal in the wonderful energetic universe. All have a story to tell.

Section 1: Transition Accounts

Note: *Peter's questions are printed in italic script.* Answers and narrative are printed in roman type.

Countrywoman

(Marie Claire lived on a farm in Normandy, northwestern France, where she was born a hundred years ago. She said she had been chosen by the Masters to represent all those people who had "a very long, productive life and a slow transition.")

Marie Claire, please tell us about your life before you died.
The long and productive part of my life was that I was raised in a small village and had a very happy childhood. In that village everyone knew everyone else. My family mostly grew crops; we also had a granary and provided milling services for a lot of the local farmers. We were on a very pleasant little stream that drove the mill for the granary.

I was one of five children and had one sister and three brothers. I was right in the middle with two older brothers, then me, then my younger brother. My sister was the baby. As we were growing up, all of us were involved in either the farm or the granary, or in taking care of the house as our mother had ill health after the last baby was born.

We lived on a commercial road and there were always some folk passing through town, so we had a constant influx of visitors. My dear Pierre, my husband, was from the same locality.

How old were you when you first met Pierre?
I knew Pierre from as far back as I could remember. We used to play together when we were children. His family had dairy cows in the area and they lived not too far from us. We used to meet in the Catholic church and went to meetings and did everything together. Pierre was the age of my elder brother, so he was several years older than me. We got married quite young by modern standards. I was 16 and he was 20. (I was born in 1901.)

Was Pierre involved in the First World War?
No, he was not a soldier in the war because we were needed to produce his family's cheese and my family's grains for the wartime effort. The first war did not affect us too much. Of course we were around for the Second World War and that affected us much more. He was part of the underground resistance.

After we married we bought a farm very close to where our parents lived and we stayed in the area. We produced a mixed crop of things; we had our own gardens where we grew a lot of our own food, and we had dairy cows and raised chickens.

Did you enjoy the work?
It was lovely. It was such a beautiful area (when there wasn't a war going on). Nobody from the larger cities really bothered us. It was a paradise like you read about in the novels. Pierre and I raised six children. We had four

boys and two girls. I guess you would say that I home-schooled them, as both Pierre and I had been. We taught them the basic things they needed, their numbers and reading and everything. We were really too busy for them to go off to the regular school. Then, when the second war hit, it was the time when they were starting to get married and to have families.

So they were old enough to be conscripted?
Three of the boys were in the French army. The second-oldest boy had an accident around the farm when he was in his teens: he had a mangled arm that had got caught in the machinery, so he was unable to go to the military because, even though he was an excellent shot, they feared he was unfit—so he became part of the underground.

The families thrived. Of course we were in the path of the struggle, to and fro, for France. We had the Germans, the Italians, the Americans, and the British. We had everyone who passed, hidden around us, and we provided as much help for the Allies as we could. The family granary was burned twice during the war. It was burned early on, then rebuilt during the conflict. Our farm was away from the city. Even with the conflict we were a very close-knit family. We worried for the boys who were in service and one of them did not come back, but we took care of his family. I ended up having 21 grandchildren because all of our children were carrying out the tradition of the family. [laughs] Not as many as my parents' family, but considering the conditions of the war it was pretty good. By the time I passed on, my great grandchildren numbered 42 and counting!

How long a life did you live?

I lived into my eighties. I was in excellent health because I always lived off the land. You go out and plant your herbs and your fruits and vegetables and take care of them. You birth the cattle, feed the chickens—and just breathe the air (those periods that were not filled with gunfire). It's the healthiest place in the whole country.

Pierre did not live as long as I did; unfortunately he passed on in his sixties. During that period I had a thriving business, not only taking care of the farm but doing quite a bit as a nanny for the children and the grand... not my children, they were big by that time—but for the grandchildren and the great-grandchildren. There were always little ones around, and there was always another generation excited about watching plants grow, playing with the bugs around them, and getting rid of the bad bugs. It was a very delightful lifetime.

When you got into your eighties, did your health decline or did you stay active to the end?
I was active until the last six months of my life. It just... my body wore out! Some say that I didn't always treat it the best. I had picked up that habit of smoking that was so prevalent among people during my lifetime. I did love, first a good cigarette and then, towards the end, a good pipe— which people indulged me. After so many years of bending over, tending the crops, picking up the eggs, and taking care of everything, my body got to the point that it did not want to straighten out once it bent over. The insides started making clicking noises instead of running as a smooth machine, and there wasn't anybody who could really figure out exactly what was wrong.

I always had the family around and they told me towards the end that they were so grateful for what I had given them and for the various experiences they had shared with me. It was with some reluctance that I realized it was time to think about moving on and not fighting any longer. In the last six months it got to the point that I had trouble getting out of bed. Then I had what some said was a stroke, where the whole right side of my body stopped functioning.

You described earlier attending church. Did religion play a part in your last years?
Religion was a comfort and a solace to me. The local priests were very accommodating during my last days. They visited frequently with communion, and sat and talked with me about how great it would be to go to heaven and to be with Pierre again, and that I did not need to suffer. It was strange that everybody thought that I was suffering. I associate suffering with pain, and the only pain I had was the mental pain of not having my body operate the way I wanted it to. I had very little physical pain. It was just like everything had stopped, but it had disconnected itself so that I did not feel it. The pain was in not being able to get up and go outside.

Take me to the day of your death.
It was a Sunday and everybody in the house had gone off to mass, which I had encouraged. I told them to pray that I would soon be with Pierre. As I was lying in bed, saying the rosary, Pierre came to me. He said, "Marie Claire, it might help at this time if we got together again. It is time to hold hands and walk through the early morning mist and fields of daisies. Are you ready?" And, of course, I was. The next thing I knew was that I leaped into his arms and he carried me, twirling me, through the fields. And we went into the Light.

Did you stay behind to go to the funeral?

7

Well, we both looked in at the funeral. While I had been aware a number of times of Pierre coming, he wasn't terrifically up to date with all the grandchildren and great-grandchildren. So at the funeral I pointed out each one and told him their peculiarities [laughs] so that in the time afterwards we would be able to visit them and see what family characteristics they carried on.

Let's go back to the moment you were in his arms. What happened to you when you got back Home?
When I got Home, I realized first that I had thought I was going to heaven, because that was what my eighty-plus years had prepared me to enjoy—the pearly gates and the big introduction to St. Peter. Instead, Pierre and I went waltzing through a place that looked exactly like where we had courted out in the fields, and we both were of that age. As we talked about our life together we would age as we talked. If we talked about what happened at the birth of one of the children, that's how old we were. If we talked about the war, that's how old we were. It was amazing— we could be whatever we wanted to be, in whatever situation we wanted, and so we re-lived our history together.

Then I began to remember, as I met some of my friends and soul mates, that religion was just a mind-set which I had in that particular lifetime, that "Home" was my true home. Home was where I existed, not only as Marie Claire but as a multitude of people whose lives I had lived. I began to examine all the lessons I had learned about dealing with family members and inter-family communication and giving of self that had been my life-lessons as Marie Claire. I began to compare those lessons with things which I had learned in other lifetimes, because my records were open and now I had the full wisdom of everything that had come before.

How many lives have you had?
Well, it's in the hundreds. I guess that's too many lives for some people. It never mattered to me or my friends how many we had or how we shared together the experiences we had. Pierre is a soul mate of mine, someone with whom I have shared other lifetimes. That is why this life was so powerful; we had decided to share a lifetime where we had a microcosm of all the relationships you can have within a family. That was why we had such a large family, so that we could deal with all the intricacies of the emotions of many people at once, trying to balance the way we dealt with, and what we could learn from, everyone else.

Do you still see Pierre?
Because he is a soul mate I see him quite a bit. It's not as if we are a couple as we had been on Earth; that was just one lifetime. In other lifetimes we lived together, we were antagonists, out-and-out enemies. It was what we had sought to learn in each particular lifetime.

What are you doing now?
I'm preparing to come back. For a while I looked in on all the kids to see what they were doing and to see if there was any way I could help them. I began to sense that I would like a life where I might influence people in some kind of teaching capacity, one which is more into dealing with people's emotions. So I haven't quite decided if I will be something like a psychiatrist, a psychologist, a minister, or a guru, but it's going to be where I have that type of an influence on people.

Thank you, Marie Claire, for telling us how you died.
I hope that this will let people know of the varied experiences they can have.

How I Died (and what I did next)

Bushman

(Lambutu, who said his name had the meaning "of the land," was a 56-year-old bushman from northwest sub-Saharan Africa. He and his family had their home in a tiny village and he had never lived near any large settlement. He described the terrain as having some hills, but it was mostly flat semi-desert. Small in stature, but genetically larger than men in so-called "pygmy" tribes, he was just under 5 ft. [1.5 m.] but very muscular.)

Tell me about your family life, Lambutu.
My family had lived off the land since before my father's fathers. We were one with the land. I felt the vibration of the land. I was a hunter, a provider. My family was my mate and our two children, a boy and a girl, and our grandchildren. Because of the land's harshness we did not have large families. Many children died as they were born or soon after birth. We had heard and knew that there were large villages of people quite a distance from us but we did not interact with them.

What sort of animals did you hunt?
The fleet of foot, both the "friendlies" and the predators. Friendlies were the cattle, gazelles, and that sort. We hunted the predators, lions and cheetahs, only when the grazing animals were unavailable. We also ate reptiles, snakes, some lizards, and in bad times we ate the larvae of insects that were around. Recently, just before my transition, we had a very bad drought and food was very

11

limited. I was having to go farther and farther away from my village to find things to bring home.

What were the highlights of your life?
I loved music. I played both the drum and the pipe—a long, hollow piece of wood with finger holes. I liked to marry and bring out the music of the land and the music of the energy that flowed through me, and to tie up the story of all creation and of the life cycle from birth to joining the grandfathers. As was common, I was married in my teen years. My children now had children, and there were three little ones, my great-grandchildren, around the house.

Did you live in a village?
Yes, in a small village. There was a series of small groups of people spread over a very large area because of the lack of food. We got together in the good times so our children could find mates from the other tribes. Our son lived in our tribe with his family and my daughter went to her husband's tribe. We were a peaceful people. We did not war on our own kind. We only tried to war on the animals for the purpose of getting food.

Did you have much contact with the white man?
Not at all. I saw one once when I was small, then my family moved even farther away from the places where they traveled. We did not like to deal with them. They were mainly interested in trying to find the stones that they called gems. People said they tried to get us to help them hunt the animals—but that was our food, our life. They hunted only for the sport of killing the animal. We respected the animal as a source of life for us.

When I was out hunting I used a weighted throwing instrument, a spear, and sometimes a bow and arrow. When it was difficult getting some of the smaller animals, I

12

would set a snare along their pathway to grab their little foot.

What else did you eat?
Roots, the tender shoots of the season. My woman planted some tubers which we harvested. They were very much like yams. So we had those. There were not a lot of berry bushes anywhere near us because our land was so dry. There were occasional trees with nuts, but we were in a desert area.

What clothing and decorations did you wear?
We used animal skins for most of our clothes. We stitched them. Because the temperature was warm, most of the time we didn't need a lot of clothing. We sewed skins together to cover ourselves up at night.

Decorations were used when we had music, and at our festivals. We used different colors of pigment from the earth to decorate our faces and bodies. As permanent markings to commemorate first kill and other important events in our lives, we placed pigment under the surface of the skin on the face—what you would call tattooing.

You enjoyed music. Were you ever a musician in a past life?
Yes, I was, but the type of music was far removed from the music in this past life. I was involved with symphonic music in Europe. I was a member of the violin section of a symphony orchestra in Vienna. Then the music was connecting with the air and the dynamics of life as it existed in Vienna. My music in the bush was connected with the pulse of the planet Mother Earth.

Lambutu, please will you now describe the situation you were in when you died?

I was out hunting for the village, and I had tracked for many days a small herd of gazelle. I was getting close enough that I was going to be able to bring one down with my throwing stick and then use my spear to dispatch it, when something startled them. I'm not sure exactly what it was but they started running towards me. I did not want to be trampled so I jumped to get out of the way. I had been crouching behind an old tree trunk that was lying on the ground and I caught my leg and it snapped. The bone protruded out through the skin. I was unconscious for some period of time. When I came to, I had lost a large amount of blood and, in addition, I was not able to support my weight on the leg at all. I was 56 years old. I was all alone. I was three or four days away from my village.

I tried to find some way to treat my leg so it would allow me to move and then I could try to find someone. I did not think that I would be able to make it all the way back to my village, but I knew some places where there might be other villagers, because they had been there at other times. I only had a few straps with which to attempt to tie a piece of a branch alongside my leg to give it some support, but my leg was swelling so badly that I could not move it very much. I had become extremely weak from having lost so much blood, and I kept on passing out. As I passed out I would see my family. At times it was almost as if they were there with me, telling me that they supported whatever I wanted to do—but I didn't know what they meant.

You found out later?
I found out from the spirits, my grandfathers, that my family was allowing me to leave because there was no way my physical body could survive what I was going through.

Did you have any food to sustain your life?

14

I had very little with me. I had had some dried meat and a bladder full of water, but it was almost gone and I could not get to a source of additional water. So my biggest problem was being out in the burning sun and not having water.

Tell me about your death.
After the beginning it was not painful. I drifted in and out of consciousness. I clung to my life for a long time, not wanting to give up because I had never given up before in that lifetime. I had always found a way to survive, to be able to go forward. As I was in and out of consciousness, my grandfather came and visited me from the Other Side and told me they were waiting for me. I didn't have to go on trying to hold on because there was a place waiting for me, but it was my choice as to when I came—whether I chose to come then or several days from then, or whether I went through the entire process of dying.

I had become very feverish because my leg had become infected. At night, in my dreams, the energy of my current family came and visited me and told me that I had been a good provider and that it was time for me to move on. I did not have to wait for them to find me. If I wanted to I could go with my grandfathers then, they assured me that they would be fine without me. This was what allowed me to cut loose of the connection my soul had to my body. The spirits of my son and daughter said they would take care of my wife, and that I did not have to worry about that.

It was very peaceful and I just changed. As I went with my grandfather it was like being a bird that rose up from the ground. I saw what had been my body and it looked horrible. Yet I felt great. I felt elated. I felt fantastic and was able to look in on where my family members were and assure myself that they were all right. I hugged my wife. One of my great-grandchildren, little Butu, saw me and he waved goodbye. Then I was with the spirits, all of the grandfathers.

Was there a rite of passage?
My passage was done gradually as I was trying to get my body to move and to sustain itself. In my unconscious state and my dream state I saw everything that had been my life, everything I had done. I became aware of the lessons I had learned. My grandfather and my other helpers, whom you would call my counselors, were there assisting me to concentrate on the things that were important.

Did this happen before you died?
It is hard to assign a time frame because towards the end there was only the tiniest fragment of my soul that was connected to my body. I was more out of my body with my grandfather and council than in it—but there was still that last hope I had of being able to go back into the physical. This was until I made the final choice that it was time to move on; then I disconnected. My body was to be returned to the Earth in whatever way was necessary. I did not stay to see what happened to it because it was no longer of any importance to me.

Did you have contact with your grandfathers when you got Home?
All my physical grandparents were there—only my elderly mother remained in physical form. So my father, uncles, aunts, and cousins who had gone before me were all there. It was like a huge festival gathering. They were all there welcoming me and remembering "when we did this, did that, had this lesson, learned that." It was all part of helping me to appreciate what I had done during my lifetime, what I had learned; then my counselors showed

16

me the list of things I had wanted to do and they were all there! So I became aware that, after all, it had been the right time for me to come Home because I had done everything I had wanted to do.

You speak of your grandfathers as if they were also soul mates. Is this a tribal feature?
In some cases it is, and it's primarily because in the tribe I chose for that lifetime there are not a lot of people with whom to interact. So in order to have contracts to be made with other people, to fulfill the major lessons you want to learn, we generally make them with a soul mate—so soul mates all come together. A lot of my relatives were soul mates.

Tell me about the lessons you learned.
The most important lesson I learned was the significance of energy communication and being able to feel the flow of life and to be able to impart that to others. I taught my children and my grandchildren to live with the Earth, to share with the Earth, to feel the Earth and feel each other. My lessons included that when born I was the youngest of three. We were all boys and my elder brothers made me feel that I was worth nothing. I had the big issue to find my worth, to find my importance, and to find my inner strength and not to give my power to other people.

So now that you are back Home, what do you do?
I'm in the chorus, a group of souls at Home who provide the background "music" for humankind. If in your quiet moments you hear the flow of energy through your body, we are that background music. We are the balance within the body to keep things tuned up.

17

Do you have any plans for the future?
I don't have plans for additional lessons I want at this stage so I haven't started talking about the next phase. I'm just very content being where I am at the moment.

Thank you, Lambutu, for telling us how you died.
Thank you for asking me.

Tsunami Girl

My name was Cialia. I lived in Sumatra, Indonesia. I was the daughter of a fisherman and a washer woman, and I lived right by the seashore. I was eight years old and had very long, black hair and a beautiful, olive-looking complexion.

Did you still play games or did you have to work?
I went to school. We were off school then because of holidays, and I helped by gathering gifts that came from the sea. Sometimes we gathered small fish, and clams, and things of that nature.

Were you learning to cook?
I'd been cooking since I was four. I liked to cook. I liked to experiment with different seasonings and found that different plants gave different tastes. A lot of the plants came from the sea. I think that in school they called them algae. There were also what we called the "sea leaves," which we could wrap the fish in. We steamed and cooked them, and then I used dandelions from the land with different berries and flowers.

Did you live in a village?
Just outside a big town.

Did you have a number of playmates?
There were quite a few. There were a number of us whose fathers were fishermen.

19

Tell me about your school.
It was a small, single building. Somebody came from the city and taught us proper language, and we were starting to read and write. We wrote mostly on slate. You can erase. Paper was very expensive. The teacher used chalk on a blackboard.

Did you like your teacher?
Yes, he was very nice. He made us laugh. He told us stories.

Now we're going to talk about your death.
I can go back to that time and go through what happened, like in a play.

Tell me what happened shortly before you died.
It was the day after the Giving Day—which most of our people call Christmas. Father had gone out at dawn to go fishing. I was with my little brother, and we were gathering things along the shore. I had a basket and was gathering up shells so I could decorate things with them. We had a project from school to gather as many different objects from the sea as we could find.

It was a very bright, beautiful day. Then, all of a sudden, the water started going away. As the water backed up, I saw fish flopping and I thought that I'd be able to bring back as many fish as daddy did. So I picked up my basket and ran along what was now the beach, picking up the fish and putting them into my basket. The water kept going farther and farther out, and the fish kept getting bigger. My basket was getting quite heavy because I wanted to fill it up. I went on going out gathering the fish.

My little brother did not keep up with me. He found a jellyfish that was stranded and was poking it with a stick. So he was not so far back from where the water started going away. By then I was a long way out.

Did you remember anything you'd ever been told about the sea going out?
There was something in the back of my mind that it was bad and we should run from it because it might come back with anger, but I thought that was just another tale we'd been told. It was much more exciting to get the fish and to be able to bring home dinner like my father did all the time.

How many people were there on the beach at the time?
There were only half a dozen in sight, mostly children of my age. I didn't see any adults around. After I had gone out some way, I was thinking about going back because my basket was full, Then I felt the ground move. I thought it was an earthquake because I had felt one earlier. But when I looked up, I was looking at a wall in front of me and coming towards me. It was as high as I could see, and it was all foamy on the top. I realized it was a wall of water and that the sea was coming back, and it was angry, it was boiling. This put me into so much fear that I couldn't move. The water kept getting closer and closer to me. Then I thought of my brother. I turned around to shout at him to run, and saw that he was already running, and I saw that most of the others were running as well. So I started dragging the basket but then let go of it because it was too heavy. Then I started running from the wall.

I had not gone very far when I was picked up off my feet by a rush of water, and a terrific pressure hit me in the back and slammed me down. My only thought was to swim away from it, and as I was swimming there were all kinds of sand and mud in the water with me. I couldn't get to the top and it felt like a weight being pressed more and more on me, as if I were being completely forced by somebody's pressure into the ground, but I could feel that I was moving because the water was moving. I never got back to the air but I was aware of being flipped, and as I was being flipped, all of a sudden I felt very peaceful, like there was no need to fight, and I should just go for the ride.

Then it became like riding a board on the wave, but I was still under the water. I was aware of the fact that I had gone beyond the beach where I had started, up and over the sand, past where our homes were, and was beginning to go up the hill in the water. But I was completely at peace now. I was looking for my brother, and as I went beyond the beach, also looking for my mother, or else my neighbors. I saw some of them but they were tumbling in the water with me. The water finally slammed into a hill at some distance inland, and as it hit the hill it broke the hill apart.

The water then started going back to the sea. It pulled the mud down from the hill and covered me. It felt very comfortable, as if I was being cuddled in a blanket. Then everything became quiet and very dark. I couldn't see anything because I was covered by the mud. I had the thought that I would stay there, and mother and father would come for me. They would know what had happened when they saw the water, and they would be able to find me. So I stayed there for some time. I did not have any sense of pain or discomfort, just confusion about where people were and what was going on. Finally I decided to go and look for people, for my parents, and my brother. As soon as I had that thought to look for them. I was suddenly out of the mud and on top of it.

Nothing looked anything like home. I looked back towards the beach and everything was completely flat, except for the ends of trees sticking up, that had been broken, and an occasional piece that looked like a roof or the side of a building. I felt very light and I was drifting around. The only people I encountered seemed to be as light and confused as I was. We were all looking for somebody.

Were you able to talk with them?
I was able to carry on a conversation with them but I did not use my voice. It was as if I reached out with thought: "Have you seen my parents? Have you seen my little brother?" They would say back to me, "No. Have you seen my uncle? Have you seen my husband?" to which I would have to say, "No." I recognized some people from the neighborhood, others I had never seen before. Most of them looked like regular people, but I noticed that they were able to walk through things. While they were talking with me, if they came to a big piece of debris they walked through it without even noticing they had, which I thought rather strange.

Were you aware then that you had died?
No, I was not aware that I was dead. I didn't become really aware of the fact that I was no longer in my body until the people with the light came. That was some time later. We were walking around for what seemed to be like a couple of days—you know, with the sun rising and setting. There were more and more people gathering in this area, all looking for someone. Then I heard this beautiful voice saying, "You don't have to stay here. Those whom you are looking for have either come to join us or they are still in their bodies." It took me a while to know what that meant, to know I was no longer alive. But still I did not know what to do about my parents. Then came the voice, and the light—it was something like a bridge with the light on the other side of the bridge. There had never been a bridge there before, but the bridge came up out of the destroyed land into this beautiful light.

Coming through this light was my grandma who had passed on sometime before. She said, "Cialia, come join me. Sami (my brother) is with me. Come, join us." I said, "But mother and father?" She said, "They're all right. They are mourning you, but they will be fine. Come join me. Come into the Light. Come Home." As I started to cross the bridge, her hand reached out towards me. And when we touched, it was as if my whole body became one. I floated into her arms, and my little brother Sami was there, and then I knew that I was Home.

Were there other people there to greet you?
There were several more of my relatives: an uncle, great-grandparents, and a cousin; then there were people I began to recognize as members of my soul group. They were all welcoming me Home. Then, finally, I began to remember that I had been on a soul journey.

Was the tsunami a lesson for you?
The tsunami was one of my lessons. I had made contracts with my parents, as did my brother, to leave them alone so they could deal with grief and their sense of abandonment. For me it had been planned as a very short life in which I would experience the bliss of a carefree childhood where everything went exactly as someone might want a lifetime to go. It was one of those lives in which you can choose as a soul to have rest and relaxation for a lifetime.

Do you remember a previous life that was not so nice?
Many lifetimes had been not so nice, lifetimes where I had been both men and women. But I'm reminded most of being a coal miner where I was in a cave-in. I was in my sixties, just about to retire from the mines.
What part of the world was that?

West Virginia in the United States of America. So this was just a short vacation. But it was also for me to experience that searching at the end—of going inside and feeling when I was a soul and when I could go back Home, and learning to deal with the pull of having such a beautiful childhood and the energy of love with my parents binding me tightly to them, so tightly that I did not want to let go of it, even though I was out of my physical body. I wanted to break those attachments, to feel the pull they could have, even when you are a non-physical entity.

What are you doing now at Home?
Now, at Home, I am working with people who have gone through what I did—where they were confused and, because of emotional attachments on Earth, wanted to stay connected. I am dealing with some who still are holding on to those last emotions, and helping them to understand what they are doing and what they can learn from letting go of them.

Do you have any plans for the future?
I am planning on returning to Earth. I don't know exactly, but I would like to experience being a psychologist, dealing with these same types of emotional issues but in a completely physical study. I hope to help those still in their bodies, just as I am helping now those who have left their bodies but aren't yet fully back Home.

Thank you, Cialia, for telling us how you died.

How I Died (and what I did next)

The North Tower

(The soul asked to be called "Susan," a name taken to protect relatives from media attention. Her death took place on September 11, 2001, in the World Trade Center, New York City, U.S.A.)

Susan, please begin with some details of your life.
When I was in human form I lived out on the [Long] Island and commuted every day to the Twin Towers. I worked in the North Tower on one of the upper floors, and loved the view of the city from up there. There was always such a sense of life within that building, as the rays of the sun would hit it or as it was covered in the mist of the day coming off the water. To see the change of the season from up there was a reaffirmation of life.

Did you have any fear of heights?
Not at all. I loved getting right up against the glass window and looking down at whatever I could see below.

What was your favorite view?
It's hard to say because at different times of the year different views were more important to me. Whether I could see the open park areas from there, or see the bustle of the little trucks and people down on the roads, or whether it was to see the large ships pass by in the harbor. From up there it was possible to see forever!

Tell me about your work.

27

I was an administrative assistant and communicated with a lot of people who did not have the great view I had. They were buried in communications centers, offices, and workplaces all over the United States. Occasionally I dealt with some people in foreign countries, but my area of expertise was middle America.

Did you ever get to see those people?
Yes, I did on occasion travel when we were implementing a new program or procedure. In my position as an administrative assistant I had to make sure that they were completely on board with everything we were doing and understood the procedures we were implementing.

Were you a New Yorker by birth?
Most of my life I've been a New Yorker. I was actually born in Pennsylvania, but my parents moved to New York when I was in my early teens. I went to high school and college in the New York area. I studied business administration in college. It was all geared towards marketing and economics. I took a broad range of courses that would help me move into a position where I could coordinate and be a mover and shaker.

Tell me about the people you worked with.
They were a very friendly lot because we dealt with so many people from so many different regional and statewide offices. Managers and staff would come in from these offices to train with us, so I got a chance to get the feel of people from all over the United States. The people were very hard workers; we liked what we were doing. The company was very good to us, and everybody knew they had a future there.

Can you tell me about the day you died?
I got to the North Tower about 7:45 a.m. We had a meeting scheduled for around nine and I wanted to make sure that everything had been brought in. We had a number of people coming in who weren't normally in the Tower. Our offices were—let me just say—above the point of impact in the North Tower. I had arranged to have beverages and little snacks for everyone and wanted to make sure everything arrived in time.

Donuts?
Actually in New York it is more often power bars and fruit, plus a few bagels.

Were you looking forward to meeting anyone in particular?
There was a new manager who was coming in from the Cleveland area with whom I had had some very interesting conversations on the phone. I wanted to meet him and see what he looked like. I had an image of what he looked like—I play those games with people on the phone, trying to work out what they look like physically from the sound of their voice and the way they talk. I always find when they show up [laughs] that I'm totally wrong. He turned out to be pretty much as I had envisioned him. Surprise, surprise!

What happened to you just before the plane struck the building?
We had all come together in the conference room. I was making sure that everybody had the packet of literature they needed. It was a corner conference room looking out right in the direction the plane came from. I was not the first to notice it. One of the other girls—actually one who was going around topping up coffee—was the one who

29

first looked up and saw it coming. She said, "O my gosh! it's going to hit us." There were jokes and laughter before we turned and saw it getting larger and larger. It was a point when none of us could move. We were glued to the sight of this immense lump of metal getting larger and larger as it came toward the building. We could see that it was going to hit lower down but not by very much, just a few floors at most below where we were. As it came in it was as if I was in the cockpit; I could see the faces of the pilots, and I could see a man with a grin who was right there in the cockpit.

Then there was a terrific bang and concussion; the building shook, and most of us, who had been standing to watch the plane approach, were knocked off our feet to the floor. The building shuddered for some time and then there was a series of explosions. The building had an amount of sway to it. When there were really big gusts of wind the building would sway, but nothing like this. This was as if you were on a flimsy pole being thrown back and forth by the concussion. As the explosions continued to go off was when we began to smell smoke. We were aware that it was below us, and my mind grasped that there would be no way to get beyond it, no way to go down.

For a while nobody spoke. It was as if we had all been put into a state of shock simultaneously, and our motor reflexes were frozen. People did help each other off the floor and we went to the windows to see if we could see anything, but this time there was only billowing smoke coming up past the windows. I checked to make sure there was nobody who was injured. No one had got more than a bump on the head from falling down and hitting a chair or the table.

My boss then started talking about what we should do. He said that, since the plane had hit on our side, we should go and try the stairways on the opposite side of the building because there was a core area which housed the elevators, and the stairs were away from them. So he and two other gentlemen went to take a look at the stairways.

Then almost everybody got the idea at the same time to call family members to tell them they were all right—because whenever something big happens in New York, everybody knows it. We were sure a huge plane hitting the building wouldn't go unnoticed. Dreadful humor on our part. I called my sister and told her that I was all right, that the floors we were on hadn't sustained any damage. She said it was already on the news. As I was talking to her on the phone I saw the other plane coming—the plane that hit the South Tower. I couldn't talk to her as I watched it. All I could do was watch that immense cylinder go toward the other building. It was down lower than the plane that had hit our building. As that building was impacted there was a wind backlash on our building, which started vibrating again as well. My sister said that she had just seen on television the other plane strike the building, and that I should hurry up and get out of the building. So I hung up after talking with her and everybody else was concluding their calls. Some of the younger girls were weeping. Even before we had any information about the stairway, there was a sense of foreboding in the whole group because we didn't know if there was going to be another plane.

Did the manager come back?
They came back shortly after I finished talking with my sister. They said they had been able to go down only about one floor and then they could see that the stairway was blocked with debris. The shaking and twisting of the structure had knocked all of the ceiling and the walls down. He said he thought that the stairway wasn't torn up

but there was so much debris that they could not get around it. So we started talking about going to the roof. Surely, if we were able to get up on the roof, they would be able to send a helicopter to take us off.

At that time it was decided that we would gather wet towels and place them around the doorways of the room because the smoke was beginning to come in. This was while a group started up to the roof. I elected to go to the roof with them. As we climbed the stairs to the roof there was quite a lot of debris on those stairwells, as well, that had broken and shaken down. When we got to the roof, the door was locked. We called around, but there was no one who had a key and there was no one who could get to us with a key.

By this time we had contacted the lobby area. They told us that the emergency workers were there and that they would find a way to get to us. What they recommended was for us to go to an outside office, since the main problem was with the fire in the core of the building. The building had open passages for the elevators which were allowing the flames and smoke to come up to the higher floors, so they told us to go into the offices and block the doorways the best we could. We went back down to the office and began getting towels to put around the doorways. We found them in the washrooms and took some sweaters and things of that kind, soaked them and laid them down.

People were still making phone calls, reaching out to loved ones. Most people were surprisingly calm. It was almost as if there wasn't anything that we could do. We were at the mercy of the rescuers being able to get to us. We couldn't go up, we couldn't go down on our own, so we just stayed there. We were starting to have trouble breathing because of the smoke, despite the precautions we had taken with the wet towels, so some of the gentlemen took chairs and broke out the windows to give us fresh air. They had told us from downstairs not to break the windows as that would help spread the flames. When we broke the windows we took turns getting close to the windows. We kept calling 911 [the emergency services], and the people in the lobby of the building, to let them know how many of us there were there and that we had nowhere to go. We were waiting for them. They kept assuring us that they would be there.

Time went on and people began telling each other their life stories and about their dreams, but we were beginning to realize that they were not going to be fulfilled. This was the time when all of us began to realize we were not going to be able to get out of the building. It was also at this time that some people panicked and couldn't stand the smoke any longer. They were huddling at the windows, leaning out, holding on to the framework of the building.

During this time we felt several shiftings, as if the floor was going down an inch or so at a time. We began to wonder if that one impact was going to make the building collapse, at least in the area we were in. We had an engineer in the group who assured us that, no, something like that couldn't happen, but I didn't believe him. We heard a really horrible sound, as if things were being wrenched apart, torn apart, and we looked out of the window and saw the South Tower crumbling in on itself. We watched as the gigantic building just disintegrated. The smoke that rose out of the falling debris blocked out what we might see, so we did not see its end at first, just a horrible haziness that covered everything. As the smoke began to clear was when the first people jumped out of the windows. They said they would rather have a clean death than to be smashed within the building. I never considered jumping because I had come to realize that this was going to be the moment when my life, as I had known it, was going to end, and I could make choices of how that would happen. I could choose to jump out of the window; I could try to get down the stairway; or I could choose to just sit there and let the smoke fill my lungs.

Then I had a vision in my head of my dear mother, who had passed away some 18 months previously. She came to me and said, "Susan, it's wonderful here. Come and join me. Don't go through all the fear of trying to escape. It's your time to come with me." In that moment I made the decision that I no longer had to stay there and have trouble breathing and fight for the life I knew I could not sustain. So I just went to sleep in the smoke, and woke up walking down this bright path with my mother.

Did you suffer a lot?
My main suffering was early on when I agonized over the thought "Why did this happen to me? Why in this manner?" I thought I had so much more to live for, so much more to do. But then I realized that I was not alone. Particularly after the South Tower went down I knew there had to have been hundreds, maybe thousands of people who perished in that fall. It wasn't just something that was happening to me but to a lot of people.

Did religion play a part for you at this time?
Religion, as I understood it at that time … I was a member of an organized religion (I won't say which), and I thought of what the minister had said on many a Sunday about how we come to Earth and we experience life, and then we go home to our Father. We go home to a beautiful place if we have led a good life. And I knew that I had led a pretty good life up to that point in time. So I knew that I would be going to that beautiful place.

So you found yourself there with your mother?
Before I was walking there with my mother, as she came to me, part of my religious beliefs were replaced with the feeling that anything outside of my body—especially considering the position I was in—was going to be fantastic. I wouldn't have to worry about grieving; I wouldn't have to worry about the heat; I wouldn't have to worry about the fear of being crushed or the fear of falling. I could just get out of this body and go with my mother because she had gotten out of her body and gone into that beautiful space. So I had the faith that she would take me where she was, to the beautiful place that had been promised.

Did you journey there or were you there straightaway?
Straightaway. As I walked out of my body we went down this short, bright path and I was there with all of my human relatives who had preceded me. I recognized some of my favorite pets from my life who were there. There were other people whom I began to recognize, though at first I did not know from where. But as I stayed the memory of things we had done in other lifetimes came back. They were my soul mates. I was welcomed and they helped me to know that I had just finished a lifetime and that I would understand everything that had happened, including the events of this last day—why it took place, and what I could learn from it.

Did you have contact with any of your former workmates?
There were some whom I saw gently passing on with me. About 20 to 25 minutes later there was a whole influx which came as that tower fell. But some of them came with confusion, and some of them I could see not quite coming

35

into the Light but staying just outside in all kinds of states of panic and fear.

Describe the place you were in. Was it just a light?
Well, the first thing I was conscious of was a brightness. It had been so cloudy, and the air in our room had been filled with particles and was so full of unbreathable things. That was all gone. But there was also a lightness to me—I could float. I felt no pain, no discomfort, no sensation of a physical body at all. I would only have to envision being somewhere else—with my cousin across a distance—and I was there. It was the ability to think and to be. All in this energy I was loved: everybody loved me and I loved everybody.

What happened after that?
I met with my council who had helped me plan that particular lifetime. They numbered 12 in total, but there were seven who were especially active in this particular life. All 12 greeted me when I was there, but the seven got down to the nitty-gritty of things that had happened, starting with things at age two and going all the way to the day of my leaving my body. We discussed that the end was something I had envisioned. [laughs] It was what I had referred to, during the planning stage, as "going out in a blaze of glory!" By that I had meant that I wanted my parting to have an impact beyond my one life and the life of my family, that it would have a wave or ripple effect across the consciousness of the whole.

Are you aware of the effect of that day?
Yes. We all monitor what goes on so that we can decide if we want to come back, what the effect has been of what we have done. We went out with a bang at the epicenter of a wave that went across the planet. Some of the effects were

good, definitely an awakening for a large portion of the people. It created a sense of purpose for all the people whom I had touched while in human form, who were still on the planet, because each and every one of them personally felt what they considered an insult to them and to their country.

So you are judging the people who did it to you?
I don't have a judgment at all. That's one of the lovely things about this place: there's nothing that's right or wrong because everything that happens to us when we are in body form is something that we have agreed to be a part of. Just as I had agreed to be one of those who lost their lives in that attack, those who flew the planes into the buildings agreed to be the spark that would ignite a movement around the world—the sense of outrage, the sense of camaraderie between people, the sense of knowing there is an evil that has to be acknowledged in the third dimension [of planet Earth]. Is there really evil in our world? No, it's just a part we play.

What are you doing now?
Well, right now I'm just taking it easy, talking to people, monitoring what's going on, deciding if I want to come back.

What might you like to come back as?
I think I'd like to try something more bucolic. Maybe being a farmer or a rancher or somebody who works with nature and sees the wildflowers as they come out in bloom.

Not being on the top of a tall building any more?
Not being in the midst of millions of people.

Thank you, Susan, for telling us how you died.
I hope it will help people understand the many things that happen at the end of a life.

Tortured

(Physically graphic)

Phien Yang, it is good to have you with us. May we start with a picture of who you were, which will explain your circumstances?
I am what is considered in my country as an intellectual. In other words, I had the opportunity of having a university education.

In which country?
Vietnam. I studied business and foreign policy, and became a member of the country's administration. This was, of course, before the overthrow of the government and the insurrection.

Were the French then in control of Vietnam?
Yes. During the time the French were there, I was a kind of liaison because one of the things I studied, and was fluent in, was the French language. It was thought by my countrymen that because I spoke the language I was better able to understand the reasoning behind their governmental policies.

What part of the country did you live in?
In the mid-north. I do not wish to say exactly where it was because there are still relatives and friends in the area.

When things started going bad, and there was the desire for self-rule among my people, there was a faction that started believing that anyone who had allied with the

39

French was selling out the country—that we did not look upon it merely as a job but it had become part of the essence of who we were—that we were more French than we were Vietnamese.

Were you Christian or Buddhist?
I was familiar with both and could talk with people of either side, so that my sympathies appeared to lie with whomever I was talking to. At home I was a practicing Buddhist. I was what a lot of people would classify as a chameleon, and had learned that to keep my employment, which was quite profitable for me. I was much valued by the French and I must have seemed to fit in with them.

What sort of work did you do?
I was a translator and interpreter of policies. In that position what I would do was to take proposals made by one group or the other and get a feeling for how the opposite group viewed them, so that the wording might be changed, if needed, in order to be understood by the other group. My primary employment was by the French, but I also got paid by the Vietnamese government to tell them what the French were doing. It wasn't exactly spying because it was transparently open to both groups. However, as things started heating up, people did not trust the other side and I was caught in the jaws of a pincher from both sides. Neither trusted me, yet neither one could do without me.

Did you try to escape from that situation?
I did not try escaping until the building I was working in was blown up by the dissidents, my countrymen. Then, because I knew they would believe whatever they wanted about my allegiance to the French, it seemed to be a good time to get out. Fortunately I did not have a family of my

own. My parents, brothers, and sisters had fled the country when things started looking bad. So I had to take care of myself. I disguised myself as a laborer and tried to slip over the border into Cambodia. I was going to go eventually to Thailand because I had some distant relatives there, but I was recognized at the border as I was trying to slip into Cambodia and was officially arrested as a spy.

I was taken to the government interrogation facility in Hanoi. It was not as openly notorious as people have now heard from other nationalities, such as the Americans, who were taken there later. This was before things began to really heat up. It was a quiet government building with a two-storey basement. The detention facilities were in the lower two levels.

It was decided that I must have critical information about the French that, for some reason, I was not telling my countrymen. The biggest form of proof for that idea was that I had tried to slip away from the country. So far as they were concerned, I was not governed by any laws that would protect me, because I was a traitor. Therefore they felt no obligation to treat me with any degree of respect or civility.

Was Ho Chi Minh, the Vietnamese nationalist leader, involved in this?
He was the one who had set up the investigative unit that had taken control of me once I was stopped at the border. He did not directly have anything to do with what happened to me. It was his number one, his first assistant, who was hands-on for part of my interrogation and that of the other semi-diplomats who had been seized after the French government building was blown up. They had also rounded up other people who had worked there with me. Most of them had not tried to leave Vietnam because they

had families within the country. I had acted immediately because the work I had been doing had given me more of an idea of the way temperaments were moving within the government, the paranoia that the government had, and the lengths to which they would go to prove that they were right and that everybody else was plotting against them.

*

The interrogation began simply enough with a deprivation of sleep, no food or water, and constant interrogation— done almost civilly. The main thrust of it was for me to divulge the plans the French had for ousting Ho Chi Minh and anyone who had political power, and for dismantling the military. Of course I had no knowledge of anything like that because nothing had been discussed with me. The French, as much as they wished to maintain control in the country, did not wish to take away its ability to be its own entity. My countrymen thought otherwise.

After about two-and-a-half days of my constantly being in those glaring lights with no sleep, no food, no nothing, they threw me into a dark cellar room. I was given a crust of bread and a little water. They mentioned that I had nothing to divulge to them and they would have to decide what to do with me. At this point I really had no concept of time. Later, in talking with some of the other prisoners, I was able to put together how long it had been. We never spoke face to face because they did not allow us to see anybody else, but when they weren't around we were able to tap messages through the walls. Sometimes we could actually hear those who were in the rooms near us. They left me in that hole for a number of days, and periodically I would get broth with maybe a little piece of fish in it with some rice. But I was never allowed to leave that room, nor to actually see anybody. There was a trap in the bottom of the cell door, which they would open up to throw the food in. Then they would come back after a while, knock on the door and say, "Give it!" and we were to put the bowl out again. We never got out to exercise or to clean ourselves. I had to use a corner of the room to evacuate what little there was to rid from my system.

After a time they turned bright lights on in the room and started blaring propaganda. It was constantly telling about the glory of the country, the magnificence of Ho Chi Minh, and the movement to take control of power in our country. This went on for several days. During all of that time I never saw another person. When the trap door was raised I would see a hand and sometimes a boot, but that was all I ever saw. During this period I had, of course, a lot of time to think and meditate. I reached the point of being able to bring myself to peace with where I was because I had not done anything wrong. The only reason I had tried to leave the country was out of fear of some of the radicals I had seen gathering. I was fairly confident that they believed that to be true of me.

Then, one day, they came in, put a sack over my head, tied my arms behind my back, took me out of the cell, and marched me into a locked van of some kind. There were several other people with me; I could hear chains on them as well, but they would not allow us to talk. It was all very ordered, "Do this, do that." We were moved a short distance, it seemed, because we weren't in the vehicle for very long. When they took us out I could not hear all the city noises I had heard before. There were some noises but they were a little distant. We appeared to have gone to a residential area or to the edge of the city. I was taken and dragged and thrown into an area with cages. The last thing they did was to unchain me and yank the hood off, and I was looking at what looked like a very small storage packing crate. We were outside.

A tiger cage?

It wasn't a tiger cage because it was metal. Most tiger cages were made of bamboo. I wasn't in one of those; I was in a metal container with a dirt floor, metal walls, and a very little window at eye level so they could look in on us. They threw me in, and I could touch both walls without stretching out my arms. The length of it was, at most, six feet [1.8 m.]. So I could easily lie down but without much extra room. As the day got warm it became very warm inside of these containers we were in. Again, they gave us little bits of broth, sometimes a vegetable, and a little bit of rice each day. They did start giving us a little more water while we were there for several days—and now I could tell days and nights because I could see the light coming through the little opening. I was looking at more of these cages so I couldn't tell where we were. I was in the center of a row of eight and couldn't see beyond those across from me. A number of days went by with nothing to do. After a while as I meditated I came to think that they had not believed me, that there was something more to come.

One morning there was the sound of very heavy vehicles coming into the area. Sometime later, the door to my unit was opened and this time the guards were in different military uniform. The men were different. There was a meanness about their energy. There was one on either side of me who dragged me out of the unit. I had no reason not to come with them because I did not know if they were going to let me go or what. They dragged me down to what looked like the barn of a small farm and took me inside. As I was going there I saw several military vehicles that were very heavily armored, and had probably caused the noise I had heard. There were men carrying rifles and machine guns of some kind. We went into their facility, which had different areas in it. In the center was a table and two chairs. It was easy to see as it was illuminated. I couldn't see what the other areas were for. There were three men in uniform in addition to the guards who brought me in.

I was taken in and sat down in the chair. This time I noticed that the chair legs had shackles on them, which they put around my lower legs. My arms were put behind me in the chair and shackled. A man who had officers' insignia on his shoulders came up and started swearing at me for being a spy and for trying to bring down the government, trying to sell out my countrymen. Then, out of the blue, for I had not expected it, he hit me as hard as he could on my cheek—so hard that the chair tumbled over. It just took my breath away; I hadn't expected that. Then the two who had brought me came and yanked the chair very forcefully and stood it back up again. The officer said, "Now you know we're serious. You need to tell us what type of information you were smuggling to the French, what type of military information they asked you to obtain, and who was your contact whom you got it from." Of course, I had no idea what they were talking about.

The officer then brought out a little type of whip, which had a leather handle and leather straps on it. He asked me the same questions. They had torn off my shirt. When he asked the questions I could not answer him, so he hit me every time I did not give him an answer. I kept asking him, "What do you want me to tell you? I can't tell you what I don't know." He just had this sneer on his face and kept hitting me. I had never felt anything like that. I boxed in school for a while so I was used to having contact with my body, but nothing stung like that leather. It wasn't very long before I passed out because it was so unexpected, and it was as much the excitement as the actual pain.

When I came to, I was back in my little hole. Two days went by and it was only food and water. Again I thought that maybe they believed me and had seen that I didn't know anything. So then, one day the door opened and two men were there and they dragged me back to the barn. This time, instead of going to the chair, they took me to a place where there were rings in the floor. They put shackles on my legs. Then they put shackles on my arms and stretched my arms up as far as they could until it was painful. Then the officer came in and tried to make fun at my expense. He said, "We have approached the front of you (meaning he had beaten my face when I was in the chair), now we will see if we can come in through the back and get the truth out of you." So the same questions: What did I steal for the French? Whom did I get it from? What were they going to do with it? Why had I sold out my country? With each question, instead of using the little whip, he had something longer, almost like a bull whip, with which he lashed my back. It was quite excruciating and, answering his questions the same way, I was thinking, "Why is this happening? I've been a good person all my life. I didn't do anything wrong. What karma did I have that made me subject to this kind of treatment?"

Did your Buddhism help you?
It made me think of the early teachings that you do have to pay for your bad karma. I spent time trying to remember how bad I had been. Why did I deserve this? And at that point I felt that I deserved on some level what was happening to me. Again the session ended with me passing out.

When I woke up they had thrown me on my back, which was bleeding, and it had partially adhered to the dirt. So it was very painful as I tried to get up. At that time I asked the gods, I asked the spirits to take me. Whatever it was I did, I had paid enough; take me, let me go. Don't let me go through any more of this. I had several days in which to do my bargaining, so to speak, with the gods, before the men came back.

This time, when I was escorted to the barn, they took me to a heavier chair that had broad arms. They fastened my own arms to the flat arms of the chair, with straps round my wrists and at my elbow. My fingers were forced into an apparatus that pulled my fingers apart but held my hand firmly down. The officer came in again and said that he was sick and tired of playing with me. It was time for me to tell them what they needed to know. At which point he started working on my fingers. I won't go into all of the details, but by the end of the day my fingers were broken, my nails had been removed, and my hand was useless. Towards the end of the session I said, "Tell me what you want me to say. I will be happy to tell you anything. I will be happy to sign any documents, saying anything just to make this stop. But I don't know what you want." He laughed and said, "You need to tell us." So I passed out. Woke up. They had known that I wrote with my left hand, so it was my right hand they did their work on.

A few days later they came to get me. They had to drag me because I didn't want to go back. This time they put me in the first chair. No shackles or anything. The officer was there alone. I could hardly stand the terrible pain I was in. He told me that everything would end if I just signed their document. I took a look at the document, which said that I was a spy and I had given the French military secrets; my intention was that they should take all power away from the Vietnamese for all time. I looked at him and said, "But this isn't the truth." He said, "You told me you would sign anything." I started to think that maybe

I should sign it, but before I could do that he took his fist and hit me as hard as he could. I woke up back in my shed, and later that day, they dragged me out. He said, "Sign this right now, for it to end," I said, "I'll sign it." So I signed it and they said, "Fine. We will prepare for your release from your body." At first all I heard was "release," so I felt quite elated with that. I went back to my little "home" and the next day they brought me a robe to put on so that my injuries were not apparent.

Again I was put in a truck but this time without the hood. They had to assist me walking because I did not have any strength. It was at this point that I realized he had said "release from your body." So I knew that it was finally over and that they were going to kill me, however they chose to do it. I also decided that I was no longer going to fight to live, so I released my energy for living. At the very moment I decided to release my energy for living, it was as if someone had given me something to make me numb. I no longer felt the pain. I was aware that they took me to a public place where there were all kinds of people. It was a stadium which my consciousness couldn't place. They had filled it with people. They read out over the loudspeakers the statements they had made me sign. Then I saw myself drifting away. I looked down and saw that somebody had shot me in the back of the head. It was at that moment that I realized it had nothing to do with karma. It was only to do with my wanting to experience man's inhumanity to man.

That final shot - did it hurt?
From the time that I decided it was time to release my will to remain in my physical body, I felt nothing. It was as if my life force was only connected to the body to keep it moving and to keep my heart beating until the time when they stopped the physical function of my body. I felt nothing because I had chosen to accept what they were

48

going to do. All the pain I had in my hand and other parts of my body ceased to bother me.

Tell me how you felt as you drifted away from your body.
When I drifted away I got back a lot of my soul memories, and I knew that my whole life and this experience had been a lesson that I had pre-determined that I wanted to experience. Not necessarily in this form, but I wanted to know the depths to which man could be inhumane to his fellow man—that he could so believe in his stories that the life of another could mean nothing.

Why did you choose such an awful lesson?
I had many lifetimes where I was in positions of power, once in a cruel way, most of the time not. I had experienced all facets of control over others, and others over me. I wanted to equate it to the physical essence of the body— the strength—and what another can do to a physical body and still have that person possess the desire to carry on. I went through all of the phases—thinking first, "I don't believe this will happen;" then, "it's over, I think I've convinced them;" then imagining that whatever I was going through was my fault; then to the point of, "they're going to do whatever they want to do;" and finally, "there is no sense in my continuing this physical experience because I now understand it."

You said that you had been cruel in one lifetime. Do you now see this as having an element of karma?
No, I don't see it as karma at all now. Once we are back into our soul form, as I am now, there is no judgment; there is no right or wrong, no punishment, no pay-back, no requirement that you have to repeat something or you have to receive what you gave.

No consequences?
No consequences!

Is karma a reality or is it a myth?
Karma is something that is created by a soul while in physical body. If it believes that it has something to repay, it will put itself into a position where that becomes a reality.

But that's only within a lifetime?
Only within the physical because, again, the soul essence is all unconditional love with no judgment, no rewards or punishments.

Do you feel angry towards those who tortured you?
Oh, absolutely not! It was my life-lesson and I would not have been able to experience it without their cooperation—which is possibly going to be very difficult for the readers of your book to understand. But if you want to learn a lesson and you don't have anyone to help you to have the physical experience you want, you are not going to be able to have it.

So the officer who conducted your torture had chosen to be that sort of person in advance.
Well, it's even a little more than that. He is a soul mate of mine. We have a tendency to incarnate at the same time so that we can be major actors in each other's lessons. We had agreed, when I chose this ultimate physical experience, that he would be the one who would allow me to be able to have it.

You say "major actors." Is human life a reality or is it all a myth?

It all depends on whether you are living it or evaluating it from over here. When you are living it, it's your reality, the reality you choose to have around you. Is it a reality to me now? I'm not physical at this moment, so in my present form I could not physically re-experience what I have just told you about. I would have to put myself back into a physical body. I would have to change my reality from one of being an unconditional energetic force to being a piece of that energetic force in a physical body.

What are you doing now?
It's rather interesting. Now, because of the experience I had, I'm monitoring various instances of torture and physical deprivation that people are forcing on others under their control—semi-slavery. I'm working in a way to help get that energy to be more recognized. Take, for instance, the recent water-boarding incidents in the Guantanamo Bay prison. I put a lot of energy in having that occurrence heard about by members of Congress to have it investigated.

Thank you, Yang, for telling us how you died.
Thank you.

[After the interview was over, Yang told us that his captors also broke his leg, but he had not detailed it in his story in consideration of readers' sensitivities.]

How I Died (and what I did next)

Trapped

My name was Ethan. I was a coal miner, from a coal miner's family. My father worked in the hole, my grandfather worked in the hole. My uncle and my two brothers—we all worked in the hole. It was something that as soon as you were ready, you went in because schooling didn't mean anything. What mattered was how much money you could earn.

Where was the mine?
In the British Isles. I prefer not to be more specific than that. This all happened in the early 1900s.

Tell me what life was like down the mine.
Cold, damp, dirty—the same thing day in, day out, minute to minute. You worked until all you could see, as you got filled up with black dust, were your eyes. I was a trencher. That's a person who goes in and works with the large boring tools, making trenches for the coal to come out of. So there was always dust around me. We lived by the whistles: the whistle when we started the day, the whistle when the trucks were coming that we loaded up with the coal, the whistle that would give us our break, the whistle that would give us our lunch, our afternoon break, and our return to the topside. So we lived by the whistles.

What did you eat for lunch?
Well, when I first started working in the mines it was Mum who first packed up our lunches. It was always some kind of a sandwich on home-baked bread. I liked cold potatoes,

53

so there was usually a cold potato or two in the lunch. Occasionally we would have some fruit, or if it was in season, some of the vegetables from the garden.

Keeping your hands clean must have been difficult.
Well you sort of overlooked what your hands looked like when you ate lunch. You took them and rubbed them on your trousers, and tried to get rid of anything that would leave too much of a taste on the food. Mum did wrap them up in butcher's paper, so mostly we tried eating right out of the paper rather than have our hands touch the food directly.

How was your health as a miner?
Early on it was very good. We lived in a hilly community, so from the time I could walk I was always running up and down hills, chasing my friends. We did not have any other transport besides our legs so we ran everywhere we went—to school, to town, to church. Being healthy and strong was important because on that depended how successful you were in the mines. If you didn't have good muscles, being a trencher as I was, you could not use those augers to make the trenches because it took a lot of force and power. You laid your whole body right behind it as you turned it to get into the different places. I had so much upper body strength that it was possible for me to get into places where other people needed a lot of room, but I could get in with a little space and turn my arms powerfully enough to make that trencher start moving.

Did you play any sports?
Well, we had a kind of rugby team going on with the young lads. It was more of a free-for-all, just an excuse for wrestling, tackling, and having a good time. But I started in the mine when I was 14½ so there weren't too many years

when we were playing. Everybody who could started young.

Did you have a girl?
I had a girl friend, Emily, almost from when I could remember. We grew up together, went to school together. Her people were all miners, as was everybody in the village. We agreed about everything. We liked the same thing—to go on walks, be out in nature. She raised rabbits, partly for food because it was a good source of meat. She sometimes got a little too connected with some of them and did not want them to be used for what they were bred for, but we overlooked that! We ended up getting married when I was 17 and I'd had been in the hole for a couple of years and was getting pretty good wages. Then Ethan junior, "little E" was what we called him, came along not too long after that. So then it was very important for me to keep working in the mines.

I really never did like the hole. It was just something you did. You know, what I liked was the weekends and the holidays when I could sit with Emily and the kids, see the sunshine, feel the rain on my face. I liked the air, that's what I liked.

You mentioned going to church: were you very involved in it?
No more so than anyone else. We always prayed for health and no accidents; that was a kind of theme, that we maintain our health, aware of the fact that miners don't have a robust, healthy life for a lot of years. Our whole desire was to work enough years that we could put a little money aside, then go off and perhaps buy a farm or a couple of animals, so we could live off them and not go back in the hole. But I never made it that far. All that

praying we did, and the village did, for no accidents didn't do me too much good either.

Tell me about the accident.
The accident came towards the end of the week. We usually worked 5½ days, all day Monday to Saturday with a half day on Saturday. It happened on Friday, towards the end of the shift. All that week we had run into what we called a "soft spot." That was where the coal was packed in with some softer materials. It was good and it was bad: good because we could get it out really fast, but bad because it wasn't a vein and you had to be extra careful not to go too fast ahead when they were coming in with the support beams, because if you did, then you had cave-ins.

We were working down there after lunch, not quite to afternoon break, three-quarters of the way through the day. There seemed to be some extra moisture on the ground, as if we were getting close to a spring. We didn't worry too much about that because you didn't get gushers very often. They were very, very rare. I'd been in the mines for about ten years by then. I was 25, so I had pretty good experience, but not like the older fellows. We had a team of 14 that day in the little end area we were working. We were cutting out some veins to test and see what the quality was like, and see if the company wanted to keep going in the same direction, or if they wanted us to go down one of the other tunnels where there was better coal. There are different grades of coal, depending on how compact it is. The more compact coal is, the longer it will burn. That's what people want. When they buy a load of coal they want it to last them a good long time. They don't want to have it all burn up in a flash. So we were taking out samples for the company.

The 14 men were all in a pretty good mood because that particular Saturday had been declared a holiday so we wouldn't have to work. We would have two full days off in a row. So everybody was talking about going to the pub and having a few before we went on home, because it was also a pay day. We were in high spirits. Nobody was doing anything different that I could see. What I did not know was that the supervisor had Danny cut some troughs around the side where I was. Now, Danny wasn't an awfully experienced trough man. He'd only been down the mines a couple of years and was only recently made a head driller—that's the person who makes the decisions where to drill and everything else. He had always been someone who followed up once the cut was started. He was batting down closer to the exit tunnel. I was in the part furthest from the exit, and periodically, I heard stuff falling. There's always rocks and stuff falling in the mines. But there seemed to be a little more noise than usual, and all of a sudden there was a bunch of shouting and a huge pile of dust came down near where I was and everybody started running.

We had lights strung along the tunnels. The lights went out. The first thing I thought was that someone had knocked down one of the supports near the exit tunnel and that had taken out the electric line. That happened every now and then, when they were pushing the trucks through. They wouldn't be watching what they were doing and would take out a post with the corner of a truck. So at first it really didn't bother me. I simply flipped the light on in my helmet. We all had these helmets you could light—a chemical type of thing. So I lit my helmet up and a couple of other people did as well. Turning around I could see, off to the right where Danny had been, there was a huge pile of rubble. So I thought, "Oh, my gosh, he must be buried," so I started running with everybody else towards that area where he was. But all we saw were his legs sticking out, and so we dug with our hands, pulling stuff off him. We found that not only he but two of the other men were under the rubble. They had all been crushed; there was nothing we could do for them. So we packed up to head on out. It was then that for the first time, as we looked, we saw that the area key had collapsed, taking out a line of supports down the side of the hole. We were looking at a complete cave-in.

There was no way we could get beyond where we were. So we were pretty sure that they would know on top what had happened. When the cave-in took place there was quite a noise and sound really travels through those tunnels. They also get some kind of an indication of trouble when the electric cuts out and the lights go off. So they knew the situation we were in. At that time nobody had any fear of anything. We felt sorry for Danny and the other men. You know, we're miners. That happens. That's part of why they pay us, you know, better than a lot of other jobs.

We took stock of what we had. The supervisor came round and said that what we would do was to drill a trough through the blockage, back down the exit tunnel. We had the equipment there with us so we might as well use what we had. That way we would be digging our way out and they would be digging their way in to get us. It seemed like a fairly good idea and we had plenty of good strong men to work on it. We decided to work on recovering the bodies first so we could take them out with us when we were ready to go. We dug them out and put them down a side tunnel—we were able to get Danny's drill from there and have some more equipment. We were quite hopeful at that time, figuring that we would be out of there in a few hours at the most. We were talking about how we'd tip a few at the pub for Danny and the boys. So we started working.

It was hard work, and I began noticing that, after we had been at the job for an hour or so, it was getting hard to breathe. We did have air holes in various places, but the nearest hole was beyond where the fall was, so we didn't have one in the area where we were. Our main job at that point was to get an air hole through to the exit tunnel. We knew that even if we still had a big mound of rocks and dirt between us and the exit, providing we had an air hole we would be all right. As we were tunneling through, every time we made any distance the hole would cave in again. We had been concentrating on the tunneling job but then we noticed that we were getting three to four inches [10 cms.] of water in the tunnel. I went back to try and see where it was coming from. I returned to the area I had been working in and noticed that, as I had taken my auger out of the last trough that I had made, there was now water coming out. Somehow I had dug into a spring which now was coming through at a pretty good rate. So first we tried to dam up the hole, putting some good sized rocks into it. These holes are about a foot in diameter, about the size of a good dinner plate, so it took quite a lot of rocks. We put them in matted with dust and dirt and that pretty much got the water down to about a trickle.

We were talking about how we were going to get through to the exit tunnel, and by this time the young men were beginning to panic. I mean, they were crying. Samuel was down on his knees praying. He'd never been a religious child but he was down there giving his confession to the world—every bad thing he'd ever done, as if he was the cause of all this. We kept on working, and as we worked it became harder and harder to breathe. Our lights were starting to get dim. Then we turned off all but a couple of them so we would have them to turn back on and the light would last longer. The men who weren't working were off to one side, resting, and we did this in shifts.

After we had been doing that for quite some time, with the water rising, though not as fast, I began to know that we weren't going to get out of there. And I got mad—I got mad that God would do this to us. Here I was: I went to church; I prayed for no accidents; I prayed for my health, but accepted that I would get the black lung sickness that everybody got when they'd been in the mines for so long— that my granddad had died of, and Pa was sick with. And now I would leave my Emily alone with the kids—by this time we had three. I became really mad and started cursing. I was cursing for everything I was worth—I'm not one to do that. Well, I wasn't one to do that *before* then, but it seemed so unfair to me. It was so unfair that, being a good person, I was not being rewarded for being a good person. That I was going through hell, stuck in this hole like a rat. No matter how hard I worked and no matter how hard the men worked with me, everything we tried, failed. So there was no hope.

I tried bargaining with God. If he'd let me out of there I'd tithe my money, give one-tenth of my money to the church, even though we didn't have that much. I'd go on retreats, say novenas, whatever He wanted me to do, so that I could stay with my family. All He had to do was to get me out of there. At that point (I hate to tell you this now) I even started bargaining with other people's lives: "I don't care if nobody else gets out of here. Just let me get out of here." Of course, I wasn't saying that part out loud—there was enough panic in the hole as it was. I'm not proud of myself for that.

There reached a point where the water had started coming in full-blast again and it was up to our knees by then. We had tried boring holes low, in the center, at the top, on the right side, on the left side; we had tried boring holes and pushing wood supports in. We had tried everything, and everything we tried, failed. We could not get a hole through to the air.

Was there a noise at the other end?
We could hear some scraping, but it seemed a long, long way away. The only thing that we could think was that the tunnel had collapsed a lot further than we had thought. The tunnel we were in was not one of the huge tunnels that was used all the time. This was one that had only been open for exploration for six months, and it was only the size of two doorways—compared with the main area where the mine had been open for centuries, or so it seemed, and was like huge rooms.

Take me to your death.
I think that because of my anger, I was one of the last to go silent. It seemed as if the younger men went first. They had given up hope, and they had just sat down and became quiet. Jimmy even went over and sat down with Danny's body because they'd been friends.

He didn't come back but was completely quiet. My anger kept me going. I was so mad at God for putting me in that position. I was there after everybody else went quiet. By this time I'm freezing as the water's almost up to my waist. As difficult as it was to move, I started pacing to and fro from where the cave-in was to where the water was coming in. I was telling the water to stop and that if God could help Moses part the Red Sea, He could stop the water from coming in so I wouldn't drown. It seemed that everything I did was being mocked or shunned. I began thinking then and there that I didn't want any part of this God. I did not want to be where He was if He was so nasty, mean, and hateful. Finally, I was exhausted and found a rock that kept me mostly out of the water—at least my legs were in the water but my bottom wasn't. I sat down there, put my back against the wall, and seethed with anger.

    I don't know if I fell asleep, or my mind wandered, or what, but my grandma came to me. Now Grandma had been gone a good five years, but there she was just like the last day I had been in her kitchen. She had her apron on when she came in, and there was the smell of baking bread and pies around her, and she was wiping the flour off her hands onto her apron. She said, "Ethan, don't you want to come and see me? Don't you want to sit down by the stove and talk about old times?" I said, "How can you put up with this? It's not fair!" She took my hands—I could almost feel it; I could feel her energy if not her flesh. Then she said, "Ethan, go inside of yourself; go into your heart and feel that love that you had for me, that you have for Emily and the children. That is what you have called God but is the true presence of God. That is the energy of the Source that is all, and which we all are. It is what the priests call the soul." Then I went into that energy, and a huge light came on, and the whole cave was lit up with light. I saw my grandpa, other relatives, and friends who had gone out in accidents in the hole or who had lived their lives in other ways and had moved on. I realized that what had so recently been in my heart, the anger and the fear, was simply something that I had wanted to experience so that I would know the depth of the love that was with them. Then I floated on up, arm in arm with Nanny. Now that I'm at Home, I know that few hours that I spent in the tunnel was the only time in that human life where I really felt the extremes of hatred and fear. It was really so valuable to me because of the sweet appreciation now of being at Home.

Then God did not hate you?
For God to have hated me would have been for me to hate myself. And in that experience was some of that as well,

because what did pass through my mind was the question why did I have to go into the mines? Why did I have to be with that particular team? Why did I have to go to work that day? And, of course, the whole answer to everything was that I had decided beforehand that I wanted to experience it.

Thank you, Ethan, for telling us how you died.
I hope that others will get a sense of the extremes that your life brings you at your own request.

How I Died (and what I did next)

Pedestrian

Paul, tell us your story.

Well, my name was Paul and I was born in a suburban area in Alberta, Canada. My parents were quite wealthy. We had a palatial estate. There was just my brother and I. We went to private schools and had everything that we could possibly need or want—and I was something of a snob. I was very proud of the riches that the family had, and I would lord it over some of those who didn't have money.

When I went off to university, Charlie, my roommate was on scholarship. And in addition to being on scholarship, he was also enrolled in a work-and-study program in order to have enough money for books, because his scholarship didn't cover his books. For the first time I was living day-to-day with somebody who not only didn't have money, but knew the value of money. I had no idea what money meant because it was always plentiful. Charlie let me see another side of the world that I had never seen. While I had no idea what I was going to do when I went off to university. I had kind of thought I might take business administration because my father had an accounting firm. But then, because of him, I decided that I wanted to learn more about other people and their struggles, so I switched into sociology—aiming to go into social work.

Charlie helped me by taking me to places where people lived on the street. It was my first brush with soup kitchens and overnight flop houses and things of that nature. What really impacted me was the young boys who had nowhere to go. A lot of them were locked out of their houses during the day, while their parents were at work, and didn't get in until after their parents came home, and just roamed the street until then.

Which city was this in?
This was in Calgary. Experiencing this was like my heart was opening. What could I do for these boys? I saw that they had no direction, they had no way to express themselves. They had all this energy, but since they didn't have anything constructive to put it into, they put it into destructive things, like breaking windows and stealing. The idea came to me that what they needed was a center that they could go to whenever they couldn't go home or whenever nobody was at home for them. It could be a place where there were physical activities so they could get rid of their excess energy, but also there would be tutoring programs and job training. There would be a way that they could get access to computers so that they might see what else was going on in the world.

This is all very well: it sounds very exalted. But it reminds me there are a lot of do-gooders in the world. Would you say that at that stage you were a do-gooder?
Probably that's how the majority of people would classify me. And considering I came from being a snob to being a do-gooder, it was, for me, a lesson in being able to see both sides of the coin. From being solely centered on myself to knowing that there were other people I could interact with, and other people whom I could help. Because of this conviction, I also became very involved in the politics of the area, because I needed support in order to put together this center that I wanted. There was a lot of negativity surrounding an idea like this because the city thought they

had enough do-good programs in the area. But they had nothing for young teenagers.

Was this just a social idea or was this also a religious conviction on your part?
It had nothing to do with religion. It was just trying to provide a way out for these kids. I saw that they were in a pattern of spiraling down and down and down by not having the same opportunities I had enjoyed as a youth, and by not having someone who cared about them at all. They were like throw-aways.

Were they from racial minorities?
Some, but it was right across the sociological board. It wasn't as much of a racial thing as it was an economic thing. There were, of course, a lot of single-parent families that these kids came from. Mostly they had single mothers, but we had two boys who were being raised by their fathers. And in every case, these parents worked so much that they weren't available for the boys. This all felt to me like it was the reason why I was on the planet. And now I know it was partially a set-up... [laughs] but I'll get to that later. So, finally, I had everything planned. I had the land for the center, I had corporations lined up to underwrite the cost. We'd had very successful fund-raising events and we were about to break ground for the center.

Were you still in college or had you graduated?
Oh, no, no. I was out of college by then, but I didn't have to work at a regular job because I had a trust fund. The day that the ground-breaking was supposed to be, there were about two hundred boys there. We had all of the officials from the city who, of course, were taking credit, but I didn't care. The anticipation was high and I was totally

caught up in the moment of the beginning of a total change for these people.

I was running late so I got out of my car when I saw everybody ready, and without looking, I ran across the street right in front of a bus. The next thing I knew I was floating above the scene watching everybody's horrified expressions. And I couldn't understand what they were horrified about until I looked down and saw my battered, mangled body.

Had you no concept of being hit?
None whatsoever. It was just ... I was rushing across the street and the next minute I was above the scene. There was no pain, there was no awareness of the bus. It was just "snap your fingers" and there was a change of scene. Then I began to run through my head what my death meant to those people down there. You know, who was going to take up the mantle of getting the center built? Who was going to constantly be knocking on doors and calling people to get things moving? I had had help in the preparation, but it was all only done at my prodding. There was no one taking initiative to do anything. Then I realized that I was going back Home and now, watching things from above, I began to remember contracts I had made with some of the souls of the boys.

Were these contracts made before you incarnated?
Yes, the contracts were for them to find the dynamic energy within themselves, so that they would change from being afraid to even say "hello" to you, to being able to get up and go. They would step in and push the same people—the politicians and the corporate bosses—to fulfill the agreements that had been made with me. And for the first time some of these boys would step up and know that they could make a difference.

These were the older boys?
Yes, they were the older boys. These were the 17- to 19-year-olds. The center was set up to help boys up to about the age of 21: the younger ones with their studies and the older ones with getting into universities or into programs where they could have job training, and for preparing them to be able to live on their own.

Did you have contracts with people in the corporations as well?
The contracts I had with those people were mainly around their integrity—whether or not they would follow through with what they had promised when the only person who really had done the handshake with them was me and I was gone.

Were you tempted to stay around rather than to go home?
Well, I was tempted to be there to hold people's hands and to kick some butt if I had to.

Did you try to do that?
I did for—I guess it was a period of seven to ten days. I was there, because everything was just dropped when I transitioned. And I knew that if things weren't immediately restarted, everything that had been done would just evaporate.

Did people actually listen to you when they were in your presence?
There were some who seemed to. There was one old curmudgeon of a corporate executive who was going to have memory lapses concerning our agreements, and I sort of made my presence known. There were some very nice testimonials to what I had done in the newspaper. And I

arranged on several days for the articles to find their way to be open on his desk when he came in. So he definitely got the idea that there was something, some energy around. And he did then fulfill the agreement he had made with me.

There was another person, a young woman who had volunteered to do some work when I was sending out flyers to people. She had a lot of her own self-confidence issues. When she saw (because she was privy to the communications that had gone back and forth) that some of the people were backing out, she became like a tigress and pushed them to stand their ground. There were a lot of transformations that took place.

With the boys, those who had always shrunk into the background, they knew this was what they needed for change not only in their lives, but in their younger brothers' and their friends' lives. So they became like a phalanx that just marched into society and said, "You have to recognize us. If you set things up for us, we will take care of ourselves and those beneath us. You don't have to be there holding our hands. Just give us a start."

You seem to be consumed still by the work that needed to be done. Was there anything you needed to do for yourself at that stage?
In my debriefing process when I went Home, my council and I talked about the shifts I had made. That lifetime for me was all about money, privilege, egotism, and being aware of the emotions generated by money and power. I went from a place of having everything to a voluntary place of taking care of those who had nothing. And within that, I learned what was important and what wasn't.

And this realization came to you after you took the step to go Home? Can you tell us about the journey there?

Well, going Home was effortless for me. One minute I'm in the physical body and the next minute I'm in the energetic, totally in the energetic body. While my thoughts and desires kept me close to the body for a short period of time, even during that time I was going back and forth from concern for the physical scene to the evaluation of what my life had been.

So you were not held entirely in the fourth dimension; you left Earth's dimension and you were, in fact, floating between the fourth and the fifth dimensions?
Yes, I did not hold on to the third, on to the physical. It was not as if I had so attached myself to something there that I could not withdraw.

Was your ability to do so because you had already been through that process and remembered what it was like in a previous life?
Now that I look back, yes, that was the reason. Because I had had a number—hundreds—of lives. And there is something that is triggered in the little soft voice in the background of your existence, saying: "You've done this before; just go with the flow," which kept moving me away from the physical. Once you leave the physical body, there's a freedom. There's a sense that there are no longer any restrictions, no longer impossibilities. The normal urge is to go with the total expanse rather than stay confined within the restrictiveness.

Now that you're completely on the Other Side, do you monitor what is going on in Calgary?
Absolutely! That's my project! [laughs] But it's more than that. I monitor the various contracts that I made with the other souls to see how they have progressed with them.

71

Do you have any ability to influence them?
I can send my energy to them. One or two of them seem to be very receptive to my energy. And there's one of the smaller boys who still asks, "What would Paul do?" [laughs] And then I try to send him the energy of what I would do. And I do believe he hears me.

Paul, thank you very much for telling us how you died

Distiller

My name was Sergei. I was born into a workers' family outside of Minsk in the Soviet Union about fifty years ago. My father worked for the railroad and my mother in one of the factories. There were the two of them, my elder brother Dmitri, and me. It was after the war but during the Cold War hostilities and the government was very much in charge of every aspect of our lives.

How did that affect you?
Immediately it did not have much effect on me, but my parents worked very, very hard for very little money. We lived in a flat in a high-rise building. There were two rooms. We shared a bathroom with only one other flat, so we were better off than most people. My brother and I went to school, of course. Everybody had to go to school. In the early years, mostly what we learned was propaganda about how great the government was, and how well they were taking care of us, and how the power was in the people. Our parents very definitely believed all that. As I got into my teen years, the people of my parents' generation began to develop an apathy. The prices of everything were continuing to go up and their wages weren't increasing as much as inflation.

My brother went out and started working. He gathered junk, anything he could find to sell. He also became a little involved with some of the roughnecks, the area thugs. He was six years older than me and I was very impressed with everything about him. When I was about 8,

73

he used to let me tag along when he was making some of his deliveries at that time. At 14 he was free enough to go anywhere and not be questioned by anybody. Even though we had identity cards that we were supposed to show everywhere, us kids never got stopped; they just let us through.

Over the next two years things continued to get more bleak. My father got hurt in the railway yards and couldn't work. He got some disability pay but it wasn't as much as he had been making, so things became extremely hard around the apartment.

Was your mother still going out to work?
Yes, in the factory. It was a clothes factory where she sorted garments. She wasn't able to maintain the house, take care of my father, and go to her job every day, so my brother found ways to bring in more money. But we still weren't able to keep up with the rent on the flat so we had to move out. We moved in with my aunt. She lived on the edge of the town in what they called a farm, although in those days she was a tenant on the farm. But her house was a little bigger so we moved in with her. It was close enough to the city so that I still went to school there, and my brother was able to maintain all of the jobs that he did for various people in the city. By the time I was 12 and he was 18, we kept seeing less and less of my brother who would disappear for three or four days at a time. Then whenever he came back, he always had money that he gave to my parents.

Did you know what he did in the city?
I knew he had become involved with some of the gangsters who were dealing in black market goods. Sometimes he would bring us something—it could be liquor, cigarettes, or meat—whatever he could get his hands on. It was also

about this time that my aunt got very involved in making liquor.

Distilling it?
Yes, distilling it from potatoes. She called it vodka but it did not taste very much like the drink we had on holidays, though it did have quite a kick to it.

Around that time, also, my father passed away. They said he died from inactivity because he could not move around. But I think it was from a broken heart because he couldn't do anything, he saw his oldest son going with the criminals, his wife was working her fingers to the bone, and [laughs] he did not really like living with his sister-in-law.

Were you close to your father?
In a strange sort of way. There was a kind of mutual misery that we shared. Neither one of us was happy; neither one of us enjoyed where we were. It was very apparent that we were contained in a women's world, where the women were taking care of all of our needs and we were rather like pets to them. It was very uncomfortable in that situation.

After father passed away, I began to help auntie with her distillery because it was becoming a very good business for her. She was selling to all the local people. Every time she would get a batch completed, there would be people at the door. It was almost as if they would appear by magic. They even brought their own jars to collect what they called "the holy water." Because I was becoming so proficient at mixing the mash and monitoring the distillation process, she began to pay me in jars. At first I sold them to make a little extra money, but then I began sampling the goods. I found that whenever I drank enough holy water, the world disappeared—the painful world that I was in. I was in a state of numbness where I could watch everybody and all of the problems they were having, but I wasn't really a part of it.

How old were you at this time?
I was 14 when I started drinking quite heavily.

Did you mother have anything to say about your drinking?
Mother was oblivious. After my father died, she stopped caring. She went through the motions: she still went to work, she still came home. She was in denial about what her sister was doing with all of the vodka. And it was like I didn't even exist because her favorite was always my brother, Dmitri, and it was around this same time that Dmitri was killed.

What happened?
He was shot in some kind of a bad deal with the black market smugglers he had been working with. At that point it was as if mother had given up living. She would go to work every day, come home, make herself something to eat, and then go to bed. That was how it went every day. Sometimes at weekends, she stayed in bed the whole time. My only companion at that point was auntie, because we had this work together.

Did auntie drink?
Not at first, to my recollection, but then I was not too aware of things that were going on at the beginning. All I cared about was the additional money I made from what I sold. When I started drinking my profits, there would be nights when she and I would sit at the kitchen table and would tell stories about when things had seemed so nice: when my mum, her sister, had been a vibrant woman;

when my father was around and how he used to joke. We would be sitting there with a jar in our hands, toasting each one of the things we remembered and we thought made us happy. I realized afterwards that she must have been drinking heavily for a long period of time because she began to get ill and have problems with her internal organs. I guess it was what you now call cirrhosis of the liver, and she was quite pickled. As she became more ill, I took over the whole business, and when I did so I expanded it.

In what way?
I bought more equipment, because I still knew some of my brother's contacts, so that I could set up an additional still and was producing much more than she had produced. The profits did not seem to increase greatly, but that might have been because I drank more.

Did the authorities know about your stills?
They were some of our best customers. The low-level bureaucrats weren't getting too much more money than anybody else, and this was an easy way for them to drown their sorrows. I was always very gracious with them—they would get a little extra or they would get a discount on what they bought. When somebody new came they would get freebies for a while, so that they wanted to protect their source. It made for a very nice working relationship. As I got older the only thing important to me was making the vodka and drinking the vodka.

So you hardly ever left the house?
I didn't have to leave the house; everybody came to me and I would even have deliveries of the potatoes and sugar and the other ingredients. In exchange for my product,

people would bring anything I needed. There were some people who tried to horn in on the operation, particularly when I was in an especially happy mood—drunk. They would try to come in and take advantage of me, but since I had been raised in this environment of having to claw my way up, I was aware of whatever they were trying to do. So I would ask one of my police or government friends to get them out of the way so it did not interfere with the constant supply that I was providing for the community.

How old were you at this point in the story?
I was eighteen. I was totally alone because it was around my eighteenth birthday that auntie passed on. Mother had been taken to a hospital for mental patients, because she had gone into such a depression that it got to the point where she stopped going to work. At that time I had the entire place to myself. So it was very easy to do the minimum needed to keep the beautiful liquid flowing. Sometimes I almost felt, as if in a dream, that I was lying under the pipes as liquid dripped down, and having it drip directly into my mouth. I saw it as an ambrosia—my connection with everything I'd always dreamed of and wanted. It became my family, my life. It was all I ever thought about.

Did you have any personal friends?
[laughs] The only friends I had were those people who needed something and didn't have any money to buy it! I had women whom I could satisfy myself with in exchange for a jar of my holy water, but I didn't have anybody who cared about me as a person.

What was the nature of your life-lesson at that point?
My life-lesson was to realize that there was no love, and to try to find a way to connect with a love from wherever it

might originate, whether an individual or an animal. I did not even have a dog at that time. I had nothing, only inanimate objects. Another lesson was to grasp what was happening to me and to value myself enough to stop the totally destructive cycle I was in.

But you weren't able to?
I wasn't able to see anything that was going on around me or pick up any sense of my own value. As far as I was concerned I was nothing. Just as I had seen my parents and my brother treated as nothing, I had that label for myself. So I thought that my job was to survive in any way I could. As there was no human interaction of that sort, I began constantly to drink myself into oblivion.

How long did you last?
It wasn't too long after my eighteenth birthday, when everybody else had passed away, that some of my customers came in and found me totally unconscious. They -took me to the local hospital where they said I had alcohol poisoning. The doctors tried to put me into their version of detoxification. But at that point I don't think there was a single cell anywhere in my body that wasn't totally pickled. When the alcohol started being removed from my cells, which had been used to it for so long, my entire body simply gave up. So by the time the doctors realized it, my body was shutting down and was beyond repair: my kidneys were gone; my liver, of course; my spleen was about to rupture. Finally my heart gave out.

Take me to the moment of your death.
Right before my death, I was having some of the most lucid thoughts I had had in years, because I was not in that constant haze. At that point, my father came to me and told

me that the life we had shared was an example of the worst that could happen to a person, and that it was time for me to come Home and to plan for a good life. I had never been very religious, but in the vision that I had of him, he was in a beautiful light with a lot of other people whose energy filled me with a sense of loving of the kind I hadn't had since I was a very young child, when things were going well. At that point, all I wanted to do was to go and join my father—so I did. I gave up my energy that still wanted to cling to my body.

How does the energy leave your body?
With our intention that we transfer energy from the body into our whole being, our whole soul, at Home. It's like pulling the plug right out of an electrical socket, and then we are no longer connected to anything other than the universe.

So you didn't feel anything in a physical sense?
No. At the moment of death I did not feel anything. Prior to that, when I was without the anesthesia of the alcohol that I was using constantly, I felt the pain of my organs going through deterioration. And when that became too bad, instead of giving me alcohol they gave me painkillers, so I didn't feel it at that time either. My passing was very blissful, going from total numbness from alcohol into a medicinal anesthesia, then into the energy of unconditional love.

What happened after you detached from your body?
I met my father, of course; my auntie was there, and my brother. Then I met with my council and we talked about the lessons I had chosen.

What is your council?
My council is a great group of friends whom I have known since—forever. They help me to plan whatever life I'm going to live when I go into a human body. They're a mixture: there's an angel or two, some souls who never have been in body form, but mostly souls who have gone through the day-to-day things that I have gone through. They have a perception of the universe as they help me decide what it is I want to learn. They had helped me decide in this particular life as Sergei that I wanted to be able to have a sense of who I was as an individual, having to do with having love in my life, confidence in myself, self-worth issues. Of course, [laughs] I must admit that I didn't succeed in learning any of the things I went down to learn.

I did learn from valuable experiences that when you get so deeply into something, you have to have a plan to be able to step away from yourself to see what's going on, or have someone intervene who will help you recognize what's going on. In my next life I'm going to work out some contracts ahead of time [with soul mates] so that if I were to lead a life, as I did then, of becoming addicted to something, and the authorities were to put me in a place where I could cut the cycle of the addiction, I could see what it feels like, evaluate what it is doing to my life, and make the choice whether to go back into the addiction or learn from it how important I am as an individual.

Sergei, do you then see your life as having been a failure?
No, not at all. I see it as experiencing the extreme of being out of control, being so addicted and so thoroughly entwined with third-dimensional things [of planet Earth] that I had no inkling at all of myself as a soul. Now I know that in any life that follows, having even a small feeling of who I am as a soul will help me to work through my issues

81

and gain a knowledge of these experiences we go through, which let us know about ourselves.

Were these experiences tough medicine?
Well, it's tough compared to being Home here in unconditional love! This feels so much more important, so much more intense, so much more euphoric that I'm really appreciating every moment I spend in it. Yes, it was an example of extremes.

So you benefit in comparing your life as Sergei with your life now?
Absolutely. Everything we souls do down on Earth enhances who and what we are, and whatever form we take at the moment.

Do you have firm plans for your next life?
Well, I'm definitely going to have some contracts, so that if I fall into a deep pit I may be pulled up short, so I can evaluate my situation. As Sergei I got into a cycle where I was so numbed and unconscious there was no way I could compare what a normal person's life might be with the life I had. Of course, when I am down there with amnesia of who I am, whether I really will take advantage of my contracts is yet to be seen.

Will you go back to Russia?
I don't know, and I don't know if I will deal with the same addiction issues. I know that what I will deal with is self-worth issues and issues of love. Of that I am certain.

Thank you, Sergei, for telling us how you died.

AIDS Hostage

(Physically graphic)

Please tell me who you are.
Ambarta. I come from the Congo in the great African continent.

Thank you, Ambarta. Can you please tell us about your life before the incident happened that caused your death?
There is a disease amongst my people. It is what you call AIDS. We just refer to it as "the affliction." My parents both had the affliction, but when I was born I was free of any taint. My father died of the affliction when I was three, and my mother lasted until I was six.

Where did you grow up?
I grew up in a rather small village, but there were other villages close by that we visited. I was raised by aunties and uncles, some of whom were part of my blood family and some who were good friends of my blood family.

Did they have the affliction?
Some of them did. The auntie who raised me the longest did not. She was the most educated in our village. She was the one who instructed us about living. The girls and boys did not go to the same school and did not get the same teaching. The boys went to a formal school in the next village, and we girls were just taught by auntie.

Did you believe in Allah, or were you Christian?
It is kind of difficult to say what I believed in, because there was Allah, there was Jesus, and there were the old gods. This was during my lifetime when everybody was trying to figure out why we had the affliction. They didn't see that Allah had an explanation for it; they didn't see that Jesus had an explanation for it; but the old gods had an explanation, and it was that we were a wicked people. The old gods also had rituals and procedures that would help people keep from getting the affliction.

And what were they?
They involved various ceremonies, dances, and the burning of different herbs, and once a strong tribal man was afflicted, he would be able to remove the curse by taking a young virgin.

What proportion of the village was afflicted?
More than half.

Do you know why this happened?
I now know, from my place here, that it was a disease that, because people did not know to be careful, they passed from person to person. Then, we all were taught that it was because we were evil and had turned away from the old gods and gone to the newer gods, to Allah and to Jesus, and we were being punished. That's what the old witch doctor said.

Were you afraid of the gods?
I was afraid of all of the gods. I listened to those who talked of Allah and how he could be so vengeful. I listened to the talk of Jesus and what he was put through by his people. And then the witch doctors were always there to shake the

rattles in our faces and threaten us with the affliction if we did not do exactly as they said.

How old were you when this became a big issue for you?
I had just turned 12 summers.

And were you then a woman?
Yes, I was a young girl—that was why I was being taught by auntie. Auntie tried to protect us from the witch doctors. It was very easy to tell who had the affliction because of the outbreaks on the skin. There were bubbly sores on those who were afflicted.

And they got tired.
They would get tired, they would get water in their lungs, and they would not be able to breathe.

Did you have to nurse them, or was that a job for the older women?
The older women took care of that. We were called "the pure ones," the ones without the affliction, and they tried to keep us separate from everyone—mainly so that the men did not know where we were. The men were instructed by the witch doctors that if they could mate with a pure, clean virgin, their affliction would be washed into the virgin, and they would be made whole. So Auntie and her friends kept the few of us who were not afflicted in hiding. They hoped they would be able to keep us there until after the period of time when we could find a pure man to mate with.

So you were indoors in the hut, were you?
Indoors in the hut, and we also had a building in the jungle, away from everything.

The men didn't know about it?
Auntie didn't think the men knew about it, but then one day, the witch doctor and a group of men, all dressed with the skin things, came to the hut we were in.

How many girls were there?
There were three of us, and we were all between 10 and 12 summers.

And how did you feel about that?
I was frightened because the men were scary, like they were possessed with something. The witch doctor had given them a potion that was supposed to be the first step in their cure, and we were supposed to be the major step: we were supposed to take from them the disease, the affliction. They broke into the hut; there were six of them with the witch doctor, and there were just the three of us. They had thought that there were more girls in the hut, and they began fighting amongst themselves to see who would be able to choose us. Auntie tried to bar them and push them out, and they hit her in the middle of her head with a machete and killed her. When we saw her fall, we gave up all hope. She was the last one who could have protected us. The witch doctor was chanting and dancing, and he had rattles and a snake, and we were all in fear.

The men battled each other until there were three who remained, and the ugliest and most scarred one jumped on me. The witch doctor told him no, it had to be done right, so the witch doctor held me down while the man violated me. There was no sense fighting because I was so small and he was so big and the witch doctor was there, so I just let him have his way, knowing that he would give me the affliction, but also knowing that it wouldn't save him. It was just a knowing I had.

86

Had your aunt told you that?
Auntie had hinted at it; she had not come right out and told us because she did not want to totally get the god mad at her, but she had told us that it would not help the silly men. The man continued to ravage me even after the witch doctor stopped holding me. Then he put a rope around my neck and led me to his hut. I was tied by my neck, with my hands tied behind me, to a post for three days, and each one of those days he did with me what he wanted.

At the end of the three days he cut me loose and just threw me out into the village. No one in the village would have anything to do with me because they knew what had happened, and they knew that I was going to get the affliction. Auntie was not around, and none of her friends dared come to our help. The other two girls who were with me in Auntie's shelter came together, and it was just the three of us trying to help each other and to console each other.

How did you get food and drink?
There were those who would put it outside the cottage; we went back to the place in the jungle, and everybody now knew where it was. When we slept, people would put a little bit of grain or something by the door for us. The littlest of us had been torn down below. She started getting a massive infection, just a bubbling—it was like when the men go out and get hurt in the jungle and then come back, and it starts to turn green. She was gone within a week after a high fever and chills and everything.

How did you feel?
I was sore and I had a lot of bruises. My arm didn't work the way it had worked—almost as if it had been pulled out of where it belonged. That had happened when I was being

thrown around by the man when he had my hands tied behind my back.

Did the man have any more to do with you?
No, not after the three days. Within a short period of time, I began to feel ill. It was fever and chills, and I began to froth from my body.

Froth?
It was like this massive stuff being expelled from me. It was sticky, and it smelled horrible, and it was yellowish-green. It was like when something rots.

From your skin?
No, from between my legs. It was not like the affliction, but it began to hurt inside of me. It was at this time that I went to see the witch doctor to see if he could help me, because this was not the affliction. When I went to him, he just looked and laughed, and he took the back of his hand and hit me as hard as he could. I stumbled backward and hit a branch on a tree and did something to my back where I could not completely stand upright. After that happened, I could not walk any distance, I now had an arm that didn't work completely, my back had me almost bent over in pain, and I lost all will to continue.

You were back in the hut?
Sometimes I could not even make it to the hut when I would leave it. At one time I fell in the street and somebody did take me back to the hut, and I never left the hut again.

What happened to the other girl?
The other girl stayed and tried to nurse me. I stayed around for several moons, during which time she began

the cough that was the affliction. She was getting weaker and weaker, but because I had trouble eating and could not move, when my mother came to me from beyond and told me that it was all right if I wanted to leave and come join her, I just grabbed her hand and went.

What was it like when you went to your mother?
I was whole again, and it was beautiful and peaceful. There was so much love, and auntie was there, and everybody told me that it was just a small piece of who I was, and that now that it was over, I didn't have to go through it again.

And did you see them on the Other Side?
I could see both sides at that point. I could see that the ugly man who had done the things to me got sicker and sicker, and as he continued to get weaker and weaker, he struck out at everyone around him and had no peace.

And what about your two girl friends?
Well, I met the young one as I went across; she was with my mother because she had gone Home before me. I watched the last of us slowly grow weaker and weaker—it was an affliction of the lungs that brought her to us. When the three of us were together again, we went dancing through the flowers and rejoiced with auntie that there would be no more pain and no more people to fear and no one to hide from.

And what did you think of the old gods and Allah and Jesus?
I think they are things that we have to deal with when we are in human form. We have to decide if any of those ideas, those rules, those ways to live make sense to us. We have the choice to make decisions. Of course, if we are physically smaller than others, our decisions may be

overruled by those larger and stronger than us, but inside, we just have to go with what our feelings are. None of those beliefs or practices could have saved any of us.

Going back to the moment of your death, were you in pain?
Yes. I had been in pain from the first time that the men grabbed us as they walked into the hut.

And did you make a decision to die?
I very definitely did. When Mother came to me in my fevered state and said that it was all right to join her, I leapt at the opportunity.

And so you switched from being in pain to being with her.
Being with her in the most beautiful feeling of love and companionship.

Did you see your body die?
I was just aware of this form lying in the straw. I didn't have any feelings toward it; it didn't have any hold on me. It was just like when snakes and lizards change their skin; it was no more than their old skin.

Now that you're back Home, what do you see as the main lesson of the life that you lived?
The lesson for me was to be in a position of being totally controlled by others, not being able to make any decisions for myself because first, I was different from the majority of the people, and second, I was so small—I never grew up. But it also was to see the various ways that a life can be lived under different practices, under different beliefs, and that one set of beliefs will allow a person to do something that is bad for other people. It was a matter also as I left that I had the freedom of choice to leave. I didn't have to stay around. I could have stayed in that body for a longer

period of time, but I would not have learned anything more than I did. It also told me that physical discomfort is just something that occurs in the body, and once out of the body, I felt only love and care.

And what was the wisdom that came from that lesson?
The wisdom was that we undertake various lessons so that we may know how marvelous, how fantastic, how beautiful, how good-feeling being at Home is, being with the love of the universe, and Source, and that whatever we go through in our physical body is just for us to appreciate more what we truly are.

Will you ever come back and suffer again?
I will come back. Some part of the life will probably have what you judge as suffering, so that I may yet see even more the magnificence of being at Home.

Thank you so much, Ambarta, for telling us how you came to die.

How I Died (and what I did next)

Innkeeper

Who are you and where do you come from?
From the Greek island of Santorini. My name is Thessala but people like to call me Thessalia.

Tell me about your home and your life.
Santorini is almost like a paradise. It has been inhabited for thousands of your years. It was a seaport town in the Mediterranean where mariners from all over the world came to trade goods. The biggest problem was that it was also an active volcano, which has erupted on a number of occasions going back about 2,000 years when it destroyed the main seaport.

Has it been dormant recently?
The last time it erupted was in 1950, right after my passing.

Tell me about your life.
We had a little inn. Santorini is very hilly, and a lot of residences are built into the hills. We had an inn of 14 rooms where vacationers and honeymooners would come to enjoy the beauty. There was a lot of work because everything had to be brought up from the road; there was no road that came immediately to our door.

Had your family owned this inn for a long time?
Yes, it was passed down through my family, and my husband came to live with us. It started out that he

delivered the bread and flour to us every day when I was young. I remember him when I was 10 or 12 and he was 17. Then as I began to get older, he always hung around our inn longer and longer with his deliveries. We started a courtship and got married when I was seventeen.

It was easy for us to make the change. When I was about 15, my father had passed away in an accident, so it was just Mother, myself, and my sister and brother. It was a little difficult for us because my brother was weak. He had had a muscle disease as a young boy and had trouble moving around, so he wasn't able to do the heavy things. My husband came and started helping us more and more, and when we married, we just moved into a house that was right next door to the inn. We were so busy during that period of time that we never really got around to having children. Not that we didn't try, but we weren't blessed with any. Life was rather hard because, as I said, we had to carry everything up, and the inn itself was quite old, so there was a lot of maintenance.

Did you have a good water supply?
Yes, the island has a very good well system that goes down deep enough to not contain any salt water

And you didn't have to carry water that far?
No, we didn't have to carry the water. We actually had piping, and when the tubes were maintained, there was no problem getting the water to us. We did have problems with electricity because the wires were old and were always getting frayed and having to be replaced or maintained.

So the inn was not very profitable?
No, but it was able to sustain itself. After we got married, we started a little restaurant, as well—more like what you

would call a cantina—that had, of course, the local beverages, but also small Mediterranean meals: dolmades, beans, things that the locals would come to munch on and that tourists found endearing. It made more work for us because we had to bring more things in and take more garbage out, so there was a constant forth and back and up and down the hills and around the pathways.

That must have been very tiring.
It was, and I don't know if I had a little of the muscle problems of my brother, but when I reached my 40s, I began having a lot of difficulty with getting tired very easily. My husband kept saying that I should rest more, but there was always something more to do.

Just as well that you didn't have a family.
We would have found time for them, had we been blessed. My sister did have four, so we had little ones around. They lived in the area where we lived, but her husband was involved in one of the stores in the town, so they weren't around to help out at the end. My sister took care of the children and worked part time in the school, so she was unavailable to help us.

So a lot of the work fell on you.
Yes. It didn't seem like it was that much at the time. It was the way I had been brought up, and it just continued. It never seemed to end. It was delightful seeing all of the different people coming from all over the world to share our beauty with us—we did enjoy that.

Would you say you had a good life?
I would say I had a very good life. It was not a life of leisure, but it was very fulfilling. There was a lot of love

from as early as I can remember, and my marriage was spectacular. My husband was always coming up with something interesting to entertain me. I never knew when to expect a little flower hidden behind a canister in the kitchen, or a little bauble of some kind hanging in the window.

A true romantic.
Yes, he was. He was such a sweetheart.

But this didn't continue forever.
No, it didn't.

Did you have any warning that you were going to die?
The only warning I had was getting more and more tired, and I thought it was just because I wasn't resting properly. I was having difficulty sleeping at night—I would wake up almost with a start, and I wouldn't know what had caused me to come out of my sleep. I had no pain or any other indication. Then one day I just woke up and I wasn't at home. I was in a place that felt beautiful. There was so much love; my father was there, my mother was there— which confused me because I knew that they had crossed over, and I didn't know why they were with me.

So you had no sensation of dying?
None whatsoever. I went to bed at night, and the next thing, I woke up and I was with my family. I thought it was a dream. I thought that I had dreamed myself into a visit with them. I was rejoicing in seeing them and being reunited with them, and I kept telling them that I had to get back because we had a full house coming in that day at the inn. They told me to take it easy, that I was with them now. I didn't understand what they meant. I said, "I can't be with you. This is just a dream. I've got to go back and

help out." They kept telling me, "No, you have joined us now. You have left your body." I didn't want to believe them, because I didn't want to *not* be at home—the physical home that I had known.

There was some period where they were trying to ease me into the realization that I was with them, that I had left my body, and I wouldn't accept it, so they finally asked me to go on a little trip with them. What we did was go to my physical funeral, and we watched as my husband, my niece and nephews and sister and brother, and all of the neighbors mourned my passing. I saw the physical body that I thought I was wearing, but it was lying there, beautifully adorned in flowers, and then I realized that I had, in fact, left the physical realm and was back Home. When that realization hit me, there was a sense of total freedom. Up until that time, I had tried to keep myself contained. It's very difficult to explain, but when I thought I was still alive, still physical, I felt the restraint of being within that physical shell, that physical body that I had inhabited, and as soon as I allowed myself to realize that my soul was free, I expanded into the universe.

Did you attempt to comfort your husband or speak to anyone?
Not immediately, because it was such a realization for me. I did stay there at the service and try to let them feel my presence, and I did feel my sweetheart sort of inflate with my energy, so I know that he felt me at that moment. I let it set for a couple of their days because I wanted there to be a pure energy when I went back to visit him. I went to him about a week later when he was in the living room office where we did all of our work. It looked like he was crying over the books, but I know he was crying from the lack of my energy being there, so I let him feel me, and with all of

my effort I projected a vision of my old self to him and thought-conveyed to him my love and that I was fine, and that he also would be fine, and that I would be with him whenever he needed me.

And have you been?
Yes, I have.

Thank you very much, Thessalia, for telling us how you died.

Playboy

It's nice of you to volunteer, Emilio—or were you pushed?
No, no—I've been watching what's going on and I think it's very important that people get an opportunity to experience different types of situations, and mine is different from anybody else's account that you have had so far.

Well then, would you be so good as to tell us a bit about your life before whatever caused your death?
I liked to consider myself a dashing Romeo, and sort of a bon vivant of the jet set. My family had lots of money, and from a very early age my brothers and I were indulged, so to speak.

How did they make their money?
It started out with importing and exporting. Then they also went into beef production and had quite a large ranch, but that was not a business that we ourselves became involved in; we just stayed in the city while that produced money for the family. The main importing and exporting was out of the city.

Which city was that?
São Paulo, a thriving city in Brazil, but I preferred to sort of go from place to place within South America, wherever I heard of something exciting happening. I would get into my little Porsche and go spinning around.

What were your chief forms of excitement?
Partying, girls, drinking, and more partying. I was in the delightful position of being the youngest and the most indulged. My oldest brother was in the family business, my middle brother went into the seminary to make my mother happy, and I got to play.

How long ago was this?
This was back in the 1960s.

So you enjoyed Porsche cars?
Yes. I had several other cars, but I had this habit of wrecking them because I would imbibe a little bit too much and then go spinning around town, and I would take the sides off on different obstacles, and things of that nature. And of course, being indulged, whenever I would get into trouble, if it was locally with the police, knowing father was a benefactor for a lot of their organizations and charities, I was just given a ride home. I could be considered quite a bit of a scallywag by world standards. I did have a very good education. I did part of my studies in Europe at boarding school, so that I had the cosmopolitan connections of the European set.

And in Portugal?
I did some of them in Portugal, yes, but I also did some in England. My latter studies were in England, my earlier boarding school was in Portugal. Then father and mother decided that I should become more of a "world person," so since I had a strong foundation in English through my studies in Portugal, I concentrated on languages. I knew French, English, Portuguese, Spanish, and a number of different languages. It was thought that at some time I would become sort of the person who would do the translation and plan the entertainment for people when

they came into town for the family business, but I never seemed to find the time to do it. Father was getting a little...I wouldn't say exactly disappointed, I would say disgusted with me, but since I was mother's favorite, and the youngest, she would always get him to produce another car for me to run around in.

How old were you at this time?
When I transitioned, I was thirty-two.

Any serious girlfriends?
I hate to say it, but I had a stable of girlfriends. I had four or five whom I could call up at any time, and they were available for whatever party or little trip I wanted to go on, or little foray. Money speaks volumes wherever you go, and there was never a lack of money.

Were you interested in any particular sports?
I was into polo. Because of having the ranch, I did spend some time there and got into riding horses, and polo was the gentlemen's sport, so polo was what I liked to lean toward. I did some other sports—I played a little soccer, but that was too much work.

Racing?
I didn't consider that a sport. That was sort of an avocation. I was always racing, whether I was in a formalized event or just going from place to place.

We're talking cars now, not horses?
We're talking cars, yes, we are definitely talking cars. I didn't seem to be able to go anyplace at a normal rate of speed. I thought that it was my right, because of my money and my cars, to have people get out of my way and let me do what I wanted to do.

Were you happy?

I was extremely happy. I didn't know what it was like to have anybody say no to me and I didn't know what it was like to want anything. And whenever I'd think that maybe I should do something a little more productive, I would just take a drive somewhere and go party.

And you didn't do anything for the poor or for society as a whole?

No. The only person who was my charity was myself. I was very self-centered, self-contained, and the world revolved around me.

Tell me what happened.

Well, as I have mentioned, I spent a lot of time in my car going from location to location, and I didn't care whether I was going to the party or coming home from the party, so it didn't matter whether I had indulged a little bit too much before I got behind the wheel or if I was dead sober. So I had been celebrating at one of the elite party places—very private; you had to be in the upper crust of society to get into these parties—and I had my girl friend Benicia with me. Benicia had been in one of my latest accidents with me when I had taken the whole side off of the car by driving a little bit too close to some trees. It was her side of the car, so she had told me that she would never again get into the car with me when I had had too much to drink. So as we were beginning to leave the party, she asked me if she could drive because I very definitely was having a little trouble navigating on my feet. But as was my experience at that time, I knew that I didn't have trouble navigating in the car, so with my warped thinking, I thought well, I might not be able to walk straight, but it doesn't take that much effort to drive the car. So I refused to let her drive, because nobody drove my cars. They were mine. They were an

102

extension of me. They were a part of me. I could feel the power in me through their engines. So when I refused, she said that she would go home with somebody else instead of me.

Did that annoy you?
Oh, it annoyed me no end. I told her that I never wanted to see her again, that she was never going to be the benefactor of any of my benevolence—in other words, she wasn't going to party with me any longer—and I got in the car in a huff. With that, the place we were at was up on the top of a hill, and it had sort of a winding road down from it, with some quite sharp corners. I was mad, and I just peeled out of the parking lot, got maybe a mile from the place, and all of a sudden I noticed that the road was turning to the left, but I was going straight ahead—right off the side of the hill. Somewhere in my consciousness I thought, "Well, I've really done it now." This was not going to be a simple little dent in the fender or the side of the car. I could see out over, and there was a body of water that the car was headed toward, with a lot of rocks, and I knew that there was absolutely no way I was going to survive that, so I said, "Goodbye, world," and the next thing I knew, it was like I—or at least my point of view—stayed in the position I was in when I made that "Goodbye, world" decision. Then I watched the car, with what looked like my body, continue its arc through the air. It went into a nosedive, crashed into the rocks, and burst into flames. I was sitting there sort of in a state of shock.

Sitting there?
It was just like floating in the air, and as I was watching the car burn, I began to be aware that I didn't have any sensations in my body at all. I was definitely no longer

inebriated, because I was acutely aware of everything that was going on. I could feel the beautiful sensation of everything being perfect, and there being love surrounding me, and began to notice light around me and soft music, and I saw shadowy figures coming toward me out of the light.

Who were they?
The first one who came up was my great-grandmother. I knew it was she because I had seen pictures of her—I had never met her when she was in body form. She came forward with this large smile on her face and just welcomed me in a huge embrace and said, "Well, now you've really done it, boyo! You're back Home with us." It was at that point, when she said "You've really done it," that the entire incident replayed itself in my mind, and I saw that at the point that the car ejected off of the roadway, the essence of me left my body.

Well in advance of the crash.
Well in advance of the crash. I had no feeling but of perfect bliss, because when it crossed my mind that there was no way I was going to survive this, I chose not to experience it.

And then you were back Home.
Yes.

Did you maintain your physical appearance?
I did for a short period of time while I went around and saw some people whom I had known in the flesh. My grandfather was there. I had an uncle and a cousin there who had their appearance that I recognized. My great-grandmother introduced me to some of the relatives, and then I just noticed that I didn't have a need for the body, so it just sort of dematerialized. But I was totally aware, when

I met someone in energy, of who it was and what their relationship was to me. It was like I was coming out of a dream and becoming aware of what was around me.

Did you look back at your life?
I did when I met with my council, my advisors. We went over all of the things that were to have been lessons in my life. As far as completing lessons, I was not very successful in that regard because I chose to run away from most of the lessons that I had. So I am planning to go back and redo the lessons, and I'm going to ensure that this time when I come back, I'm not in a privileged family, so that I don't get lured away by making easy choices, as a human considers them.

Thank you, Emilio, for telling us how you died.
I hope that this will help people understand a lot of things—that they don't have to go through pain at the time of their death, and that we do learn from the choices we make; we learn what not to do in order to learn lessons.

How I Died (and what I did next)

Hammer

(Physically graphic)

*I understand that you'd like us to call you by your nickname.
You're from Italy, are you?*
Yes, I am. I was in the construction trade. I never really
liked my given name, and from the first time I started
working part time at sixteen, everybody just called me
"Hammer" because I could take one of those big-boy
hammers and, with just one whack, put a nail through a
board.

*Good for you. You were proud of your muscle strength, were
you?*
Absolutely. I always kept myself in really good shape.

What sort of work were you doing?
Construction, mainly on family homes and apartment
buildings—residential-type construction.

In what part of Italy?
Up in the northwestern section.

How long ago did all this happen?
This happened around your 1950s.

Tell us what you were doing.
As I said, I was in construction. I had started out as a
teenager, working summers. I liked to do the outside
frame-up work, where we would put on the outside tresses

and framework. I really got a lot of pleasure out of sitting up on the roof and being able to see the surrounding area and all of the people.

It can be quite dangerous up there, can't it?
Well, I never thought so because I had a good sense of balance, and I never worried about anything like that. I was 42 when I had my accident, so I had spent quite a while on the roofs, on the structures, and never had anything worse than a splinter or hangnail in all that time.

This particular day it was really windy, and when it got to be super windy we would have to call off construction because it was just too dangerous with the wood picking up—getting volume under it and being hard to hold down and everything. We had a couple of new guys on the construction site who were doing the carry work. They were bringing the boards up and putting the prefab stresses into place and all that. I was just doing my usual thing of hammering those nails in to get everything into place. We had started using metal support pieces that would hold the structure into place. We'd bring the pieces up, and I would put a metal plate down and hammer into both the top and the sides to hold everything in place. I would be really concentrating on what I was doing because you had to watch out for your fingers. Every now and then I did slip a little and hit a finger, but I didn't consider that anything very serious.

So that day you were putting up a roof?
We were up on the top floor of a four-storey apartment house on the east side of town, and we had built all the way up to the roof. We had framed up the four floors with all of the apartments. The wind was picking up pretty fast and I was down putting the braces in, and all of a sudden I got whacked on the side of the head by a board. The

carriers were bringing up support beams, and I heard later as they were talking (in the hospital) that one beam slipped a little bit, and the wind got underneath and swung it around, and it caught me right in the side of the head, and of course it was the side of the head away from the edge, so it was coming from the inside and it just wiped me right off the building. I tumbled through the air. I knew enough to relax my body, but it didn't help that I landed on my right hip, right on top of a boulder on the ground.

Did you pass out?
Yes, it knocked me out. The next thing I was conscious of was being on a gurney in the hospital and being rolled down past all these lights on the ceiling and everybody screaming and hollering. At first I wasn't conscious of any pain—it was like my whole body was numb. My foreman was there, and he kept saying everything was going to be all right and I'd be back up hammering in no time at all, and I heard somebody screaming to get my family there. Then they put something into my arm, and I definitely didn't feel anything.

While you're not feeling anything, tell me about your family. You had a wife, did you?
I had a wife and three boys. One of them was a teenager—that was Antoni. He was 17 and was just finishing up school and trying to decide whether he was going to go on. He kind of decided he might want to be an architect because from the time he was small he used to come around to the construction site with me, and he was more interested in designing things than in putting them together. Then there was Matthew, the middle one. Matthew was 15, and all he cared about was soccer. Then there was little Andrew. He was our surprise. He was only

five at the time. We didn't really expect him. He was definitely a mama's boy, but he loved to read.

So you were given an injection.
I was given an injection for the pain; it didn't really knock me out. They were doing all the examining and putting me into these positions to take x-rays and do all kinds of things—I think they called them cat scans or something like that—I don't know. It was something new that they were just experimenting with. I was lucky that I was in a big town and they had all of this specialty-type stuff. Then I was in a curtained-off room with all kinds of machines. I wasn't having any trouble breathing, but it was like I couldn't move my body because they had me hooked up to all kinds of things. My wife got there and she was all weepy. They let my oldest boy come in with her. She was telling me that I was broken up pretty badly in my hip and leg area, and the doctors were saying that there was some bruising and tearing inside of me, too, that they were going to have to do surgery on to repair the stuff inside and put in some plates or something. They talked about screws. Now here I'm the hammer man and I like nails, and they're going to put screws in me—I didn't know whether I liked that or not.

I don't think you'd have enjoyed nails.
Well, you sure can't hammer in a screw. So I told them, well, they had to do what they had to do. Everybody said everything was going to take quite some time, but that I wouldn't feel anything, and that they'd see me when I came out of the surgery. So I just trusted them. My wife told me everything was going to be all right.

So you went to surgery.

So I went to surgery. They put something else into one of the bags that was attached to my arm, and I just remember going into this very peaceful sleep. The next thing that happened was really kind of strange, because all of a sudden it's like I felt this little pop, like a cork coming out of a bottle or something, and I was looking down and I could see my body lying on the table with all these people with these gown things on and masks and stuff, and yet I'm up top, able to see everything that's going on—kind of floating up toward the ceiling. Boy, was my body a mess! I hadn't seen it up to that time, and I noticed that it looked like the whole area just a little south of my middle was scrunched up like somebody had taken a hammer and had pounded it almost flat from the backside. It looked really weird. And I'm listening to what they're saying and I could see that they had me kind of slit open in the front, and they're talking about things like kidneys and liver and spleen and that they didn't like the way any of them looked. I could see when they split me open that there was just gushy stuff all over the place—a lot of blood. It's a good thing I didn't faint at the sight of blood, even though I wasn't in my body anyway.

What was it like not being in your body?
It was kind of neat, kind of like I was two people. I was this watcher who could see everything that was going on, but I was also the subject of everybody's attention. But I had no feeling, no conscious connection with the body itself.

So you had no physical feeling at all.
No physical sensations whatsoever. I could hear everything that was going on, and at one point in time I tried to ask a question, and they couldn't hear me. I tried to ask them what was going on and what they were going to

do. I had to figure out what was going on by what they said, and they said something about taking care of all the internal damage first before trying to work on the bones.

Could you read their thoughts?
It was kind of funny, because I guess that's what I was doing with some of them, because it was like I heard the conversation they were having with each other, but then I heard little snippets of things like, "Man, this is really a mess. I've never seen anything as bad as this," but nobody was saying that out loud. It was right about then that I kind of got distracted by a big, white light. It was coming at me from a position just about level with me on the ceiling, and it was like a tunnel. It really intrigued me because it was so bright, so I kind of put all my attention to it. I heard somebody calling my name, so I listened and I went toward the light and went through, and there was my granddad. My granddad was also in the construction trade, and he had died in an accident, and I thought at the moment, does this mean I'm dying? So I asked him, and he said that there were a lot of things I had to think about right then.

So we just sort of went for a stroll, and at that point I couldn't see any of the doctors or nurses or anything. Nono (I called my grandfather "Nono") and I were in this area that was beautiful, just like a garden area, and he was telling me, "You know, your body's in really bad shape," and I said, "Yeah, but they can fix it," and he said, "But the way they're going to fix it, you're not going to be able to walk again." And I said, "What do you mean I'm not going to be able to walk again?" And he said, "There's too much damage, and one of the things that got damaged was your spinal cord, so you're not going to have any feeling from your waist down. Also, your internal organs are such a mess that you're going to have bags, and you're going to have problems digesting food..." And I said, "Wait a minute, Nono—I don't want to hear any of this. I've got to go back to my wife and boys." And he said, "Well, you can go back to the wife and boys, but the life you're going to have isn't going to be the life you've had. You're going to just be there, and they're going to have to take care of you."

At this point, even though I couldn't feel or anything, I could feel myself start to cry, because I realized that if I did go back—and Nono said I had the choice to go back—I would be a burden on them, and that everything that we had worked for and all the money that we had put away for when I retired would go into taking care of me, and we would just be taken care of by the government. I didn't want that, particularly for the young one, because he wouldn't have a chance to do anything then. So I asked Nono, "What's the alternative?" And he said, "You can make the choice to come Home." And I said, "How can I make a choice like that?" And he said, "Because we have freedom of choice." And I said, "Don't I have something I need to do with the boys and with the family?" And he said, "You have a choice as to how you want them to interact in their lives from now on—whether you want to be a part of it or whether you want them to find their strength and go forward." So I told him, "I've really got to think about this," and he said, "That's fine." And as soon as he said "That's fine," I was back on the ceiling of that operating room.

Then I really started listening to what they were saying, and they started talking about how much damage there was, and they didn't know whether they could fix it. They didn't know if I was ever going to come out of the anesthesia or if I was going to be sort of like a vegetable, and I didn't want to put the family through that, so as I'm thinking I didn't want to put the family through that, the machines started going crazy. They started beeping, and everybody started screaming, "We're losing him! His blood pressure's bottoming out!" And I looked down, and there was blood gushing out from a couple of places, and I thought wait a minute—I'm not ready to make a decision! So everything settled back down again and they clamped down the blood, and I'm thinking, "This really *is* my choice. It *is* my choice what happens, where I go, whether I stay." So I watched them a while longer. They had done all the repair inside, and then they opened up from the side so that they could take a look at the hip, and some of it looked almost like sawdust. There were just little pieces all over the place.

I knew then that I wasn't the Hammer anymore, that I never would be in that body with a hammer, and I just said, "Okay, Nono, let's go Home." Then everything started going crazy in the room again—bells ringing and everything else, and they were saying, "We're losing him," and the light came back and Nono was there and I saw his hand come down, and I grabbed onto it and went Home.

What was it like when you went Home?
It was the most magnificent, fantastic thing in the world. Other relatives I had known in this life were there. I remember people coming up to me with whom I had been in previous lives, and Nono said, "I know you're hurting, so let's go forward a little bit. So we went to the house, where everybody was making arrangements for my funeral, and I saw how strong they were, and I knew I'd made the right decision. And then he took me forward to what each one of the boys became because of what the money from my insurance allowed them to do. And my Gina found somebody in later life to be a companion for her.

You seem happy at that.

I was happy at everything that I saw, and I just watch over them now.

Are you able to influence them?
Well, as much as a spirit or guide can—you know, just put a little thought here or there and see what they decide to do with it, but I'm there watching over them, and I think they know it.

Thank you, Hammer, for telling us how you died.

How I Died (and what I did next)

Street Kid

(Sexually graphic)

Ramon, tell us about your life before you transitioned.
I was what was known as a street kid. When I was about eight years old, my mother, who had been raising my brothers and me, went back Home; my father had left us when my last brother was born.

Was your mother ill?
It was what we called poverty—we didn't have any food; we didn't have anywhere to live; we were living in a shanty [Toni: he's showing me a place that's mostly cardboard sides with a tin roof]. We were living in shantytown, on the outskirts of Buenos Aires—my mother and my three brothers and me. We had a hovel where our beds were newspapers we had found to insulate ourselves from the ground. There was no running water or electricity. There was a pump for water about a block away from where we lived. The entire area that we lived in went for blocks and blocks. During the time that Mama was with us, the police were not too bad—they didn't come and harass us too much. In the beginning, Mother did have a partial job of taking in laundry. There was a laundry area in our little grouping, and women could go and use the tubs and hot water that were there and do laundry for people. She got a few pennies for that, and it was enough that we were able to have some bread and, occasionally, cheese or sausage with it. There were aid workers who came in and

117

periodically set up what you would call soup kitchens, and we would get a hot meal from them.

But not all the time.
Not all the time. Generally when they came, big politicians or important people came with them and there would be people with cameras and recording devices who would be there making a big thing about what they were doing for us, how they were taking care of us. At the time my mother passed on, there were those who were in charge of our little place—the honchos, the leaders—and when people died, they would come along and make sure the bodies got out so they wouldn't putrefy. Then they contacted people to make sure the children had somewhere to go. We never knew where they went because they never came back and we never heard from them again, but I had heard rumors that the children were taken to places that weren't so nice.

Were you one of the older ones?
I was the oldest of the four boys—I was eight when Mama passed.

How old were the others?
Six, four, and two. After they took Mama's body away, and I heard they were coming to take us, I told my brothers that they would be fine. I had been doing some begging on the streets with some friends, so I knew that I could take care of myself, and I didn't want to go away and disappear like everybody else had. So when they came to take the little ones, I hid. The people who came seemed nice enough, but they didn't care. They didn't take any of the few clothes or toys or things that we had. Now, by toys I mean things that Mama had put together, made from sticks and cans and things like that—little trucks and things—but they didn't take any of that. They didn't take my littlest brother's

blanket, which was actually a towel, and I heard him crying and crying over that.

When I saw that they didn't really care what was happening, I knew that my decision not to go with them was the right thing. I hid out, and two of my friends were there with me, and as soon as they had taken my brothers away, I went and lived with the family of one of my friends. Family was just his older brother, who was in his teens, and somebody who called himself his uncle, but I don't know if they were really related. They had sort of a large— it wasn't much more than our place, but the sides of the building were a little more substantial. They were made out of pieces of wood with the tin roof. They had food because all of the people there—my friend and his brother and several other people—we all went out and begged on the streets and brought the money back to Uncle. We lived like that for several years. It was fairly nice; my stomach was mostly full, not with things I enjoyed, but with mush and things like that.

Whom were you begging from?
Mostly the tourists.

Tourists?
There were a lot of tourists in Buenos Aires.

Oh, you went out of the shantytown.
We went out of the shantytown. In the beginning we just went across the road from where the shanty was—well, it was road and railroad tracks. We crossed the road and the tracks. There were big fences, but they had holes in them so that we could get through, and we went into the villages. There were some hotels right on the edge, not really fancy places. Once I got a bit older, 10 or 11, that was

when the crackdown began, when the military came in and started tearing down our houses. Uncle—his name was Felix—Uncle Felix was very protective of us boys. There were now about 10 of us, and he gave things to the police and the soldiers who came around so that they left us alone in the beginning. They would just tear down and burn areas on the other side of our little home area. That lasted for another couple of years. Then when I was about 12 or 13, they came through with bulldozers one day and knocked everything down. Somebody had told Felix ahead of time that this was going to happen, so he had gathered all of us up, and somebody came with a truck and took us to an abandoned building that had been used for storage. We all moved in there, and it was really nice because it had solid walls and a few windows and it was much closer to areas where people could buy things, so there were more people there with more money.

Where did you buy clothes and things?
Whenever the aid people came around they would generally bring boxes of things, and we would go through and get what we needed. When we couldn't find clothing, Felix found some for us. It was not what you would call good clothing, but when we first got it, it would be nice and clean. When we moved to this new place, Felix said we had to look better, so he made us start to keep our clothes clean, and he made sure that there were more clothes that we could change into.

How did you manage with sickness and teeth problems and things like that?
If anybody got really sick, Felix said he took them to the hospital, but they never came back, so we don't know. I got a bad chest thing for a while where I coughed and spit up this yellow-green stuff. Felix took me to a clinic, and the

doctor at the clinic gave me some horrible stuff to drink, and within a few days it was better. I never really had anything else wrong with me. When I was about 13 years old, by this time we were in the building and we were very close to a big marketplace where people were selling hats and clothing and food items and things and a lot of tourists came. We would be around the outskirts begging when they came in, and we started getting more and more money, and the more money we brought in, the better our food got, because Felix would take care of us, and the number of boys with us would be anywhere from a minimum of eight up to almost two dozen.

Around this time Felix took me aside one day and asked me if I would like to be one of his special boys. I asked him what that meant, and he said that meant I would get to stay in a special place where I'd have my own bed. I'd been sleeping all these years on the ground on newspapers—I wasn't even sure what he meant by a bed at first, but he showed me and it looked really nice, so I said sure, what did I have to do? And he said what I had to do was to please friends of his. I wasn't sure what he meant, so I said OK. I was given really nice clothes and went to a place where the bedrooms also had showers, and I got to take a shower—something that happened only every couple of weeks at the other place. So I took a shower, and he gave me some clothes that almost looked new, and I went to somebody's party.

There were people, there was music, there was dancing, and I noticed it was all men. I just thought they were friends of Felix's. There was a young man—I say young because some of them in there were very old—but there was this young man who looked about as old as my friend's brother, so he was about 22 or something like that, and he was fine. He had rings on his fingers and jewelry around his neck—he looked fancier than any of the tourists we'd been getting money from. He held up a big amount of money and asked me if I'd like it, and I said, "Of course I'd like it!" And he said, "Well, you've got to come with me." And I said, "But can I come back to my friends?" because I didn't want to leave my friends, and he said, "Yes, you'll be back to your friends. Why don't you share my drink?" I tasted his drink, and it tasted kind of funny and made my head kind of spin, but it made me feel great. So I said, "Hey, this is fantastic—I'm partying."

So we went into this back room and he started undressing me. I thought, well, OK—he said I had to do what he wanted. And then he went down to my private parts and did all kinds of funny things down there, but it did feel kind of good. So I was thinking well, this isn't really what I like, but... Then he gave me some more to drink and I said OK, that's fine. Then he undressed and made me take his thing in my mouth and held my head there and moved it up and down, and then I got a whole mouthful of his stuff and I thought yecch!—well, OK.

Then he let me go and I went back home and I had all of this money, and Felix was just really happy. He thought that was great and told me I was going to be his best special boy. He asked me if I liked the stuff to drink and I said yeah, it made me feel kind of good; he gave me a little bottle of it and let me go to bed, so I went to bed. It was really great—he bought me some candy and a sausage, and things were just fantastic. About a week or so later, he said, "Let's go to another party." I said OK because things were really good for me. I had never had so much food, and I didn't have to go out begging with everybody else anymore. I could just watch what everybody was doing, and there was a little radio in this special place and we could listen to the radio.

Were there any other boys there with you?
There were four other boys, but we each had our own private little rooms—it was like a house.

In the warehouse?
No, this was in a special place away from the warehouse. I didn't have to stay with the boys in the warehouse anymore. This was a special place. We even had a little yard that we could go out into—it was like a regular house. After a while, we even had a woman who came and cooked for us, because Felix said he thought we should get our bodies bigger and stronger, so we had regular food and they just kept bringing more things for us. It was great. But then we kept having these parties, and it would be the same thing—there would always be a man there, and after the first couple of times, the men wanted me to do other things. They wanted me to bend over so that they could put their thing in me, and I didn't like that because it hurt. But when I tried to cry out, they would hit me upside the head and say they would tell Felix, so I just blocked it out so I wouldn't think about it and just lived for the times afterward and all the presents and things. I started to get really nice clothes and had as much food as I wanted to eat. I noticed that some of the other boys would come back looking like they were all beat up, like when we used to get in fights, and I would ask them what had happened. Most of them wouldn't say, but one of them told me that when he didn't do what the man Felix had put him with wanted, the guy took a belt to him. I didn't want any of that, so I did whatever they wanted me to do. As I got older, when I was about 14, I told Felix I didn't want to do this anymore. I was starting to be frightened of some of the men, because some of them were really cruel. They wanted to spank me or beat me, and I didn't want to have anything to do with

123

that. Felix said he had something for me that would fix it so that it wouldn't make any difference.

Wouldn't make any difference?
I wouldn't feel it, I wouldn't care. So what he did was bring out a bottle of liquid and a tube that had like a needle on it. He filled the tube up and put it into my arm, and oh, it was like when I was going into a fantastic dream. It was just marvelous—I didn't care about anything. After the first time, it was like I just floated. I didn't do anything. I just stayed in bed all day that day.

What did he call it?
He called it "H," and he said "H" could stand for heaven or it could stand for hell. It was heaven when you used it, and it could be hell when you didn't. I told him I wanted the heaven part of it. He had started some of the other boys on "H" too, and we would have like an assembly line where we would go in and he would give all of us our shots and then we would just be blissful. It was almost like he would give us a little extra on the days that we went to the parties, and then I didn't care what happened because I was always in this beautiful cloud.

There was one time, after one of the parties, when I was starting to feel bad again, and I went looking for Felix and he wasn't around. I was really starting to panic because I began shaking and was all wet with sweat. I was yelling for Felix and nobody knew where he was, and all I could do was just huddle on the bed and hold myself because I was in such misery. Every little piece of me hurt. I don't know how long I was there—it had to have been at least a couple of days—and then Felix came back. He didn't look too good, and he said that the authorities had taken him but that his—I think he said lawyer had gotten him out. Then he gave me some of the "H" and I felt better again. I felt really good, and I told him I never wanted to be without it again.

We went on like this for about another two years, and it seemed that it took more and more of the "H" to keep me in a place where it didn't matter to me what was happening to me. Then things started getting kind of weird. I started getting blockages of memory where it was just like I didn't remember whole days—what happened or anything else—and the only thing that was important to me was having the "H." I didn't care what anybody did to me; I just had to have that "H."

Then there was a big party, and I was just kind of out of it, and I was feeling so good I told Felix, "I'm not going to go. I'll skip this party—I just want to stay here." He said, "No, you're going to go. I'll tell you what: to make you feel better I'll give you some more 'H.'" Well, I had already had quite a bit of "H" that day, but I was never going to pass up having that good feeling, so he put some more into me, and when he did, my heart just felt like it was trying to get out of my chest. It started thumping and thumping and thumping, and I could feel the blood going through my veins, and I saw white spots before my eyes, and I couldn't breathe. And then I was just above my body, looking down, and Felix was panicking. He was screaming for somebody to get the doctor and he was trying to shake me back into my body.

He didn't know I was out of my body. It was different because I felt that euphoria that I felt when he gave me the "H," but I couldn't feel the physical body. I just felt the height of all of the excitement and the tenderness and the goodness of it, and then I heard a voice, and it sounded like my mama. I looked up and she was like in a cloud above me, and she said, "Ramon, baby, come to me." And I did. And then I remembered that Ramon was just an

125

experience I wanted to have. I wanted to see what it was like to be totally controlled by another person, how it was like to be controlled also by a substance that would take my whole mind away, take away my wants or desires for anything else, and I knew right then and there I never wanted to experience that again. Anything I did from then on, I wanted to have choices, and I wanted those choices to be my own.

And do you have choices?
Absolutely. I have total choice of everything I do, and I realize that I didn't learn much from that whole experience except that I don't want to do it again. I learned not to trust in someone else instead of trusting in my own instincts that something is wrong; I should always go with my own instincts.

When you were alive, did you have that choice—to trust in yourself?
In the beginning, when things started going wrong with the setup Felix created, I could have walked away because there were more aid workers, social workers, in the area who were trying to talk us into coming with them, but I didn't want to give up that feel-good feeling that Felix could give me, and that was more important than being responsible for myself.

Do you know what substance he gave you?
It was heroin, and it was extremely addictive. It cut out all of the inhibitions I had and gave me a sense of being able to remove myself from any pain or anything that was being inflicted upon my body and stay in that blissful, cloudlike state. As long as he continued giving me those injections, I was totally unaware of whatever happened to my body.

So what is it like where you are now?
It's unconditional love. What I thought was love from Felix, and a sense of well-being from the drug, is nothing compared to what there is now. That was totally without connection to any sensation of belonging. It was actually very restrictive and confining because I wasn't able to feel anything. I felt a physical euphoria, but I wasn't able to feel the essence of who I was. I was cutting myself off from any connection to my soul.

And now?
Now I'm living as my soul. I am in contact with every incident of the life I lived. I can go back and put myself into a situation, remove the influence of the heroin, and know what it feels like and what I could learn from having experienced that without being under the influence of the drug.

That was a hard lesson. Do you feel that it was worthwhile?
For me it was, because I had not dealt previously with the situation of being addicted to anything. In an addiction, you take away all of your choices. You are totally driven by the need to stay under the influence of that substance. You live in a non-living situation where you are out of context with everything that's around you.

But now you have choices.
We all have choices. I had a choice to get out of that, but the addiction was so strong that I couldn't exercise that choice.

Are you planning to come down to Earth again?
I am, and when I come down, I plan on being in a situation where I can influence people who have addictions and try

to let them know that there are choices, even when you're in the throes of an addiction. Of course, that will be my plan if I deal with the other lessons that I'll be learning first.

Thank you, Ramon, for telling us how you died.

Suicide Bombers

[Toni was introduced to two souls who asked to be identified by their first names, Jasmin and Ziv.]

Let's start with you, Jasmin.
J: I lived in Palestine—or at least my family was there: my husband, brothers, sisters, parents. We were in the border town area in a village of very angry people. We were angry about the oppression from the Israelis and how they kept pushing us back and putting up walls to prevent us from being able to get to Israel and some of our holy sites.

I was a very accurate translator of a lot of Middle Eastern languages, and was sometimes employed by the Israeli government and other times by various businesses in Israel, so I had papers to be able to go in and out of Israel any time I wished. I didn't just work in one particular area but worked all over the country, depending upon where they needed a translator and what was needing to be done.

What sort of documents were you translating?
J: It would depend upon whom I was working for. If it was the government, it could be documents concerning things that they had seized from groups—which was quite interesting considering that, being Palestinian, I could interpret from the wording who some of the writers of these documents were, but for some reason, because I had all of these clearances, they didn't think that made any difference.

129

Were you a supporter of Hamas?
J: I wasn't in the beginning. My husband became a supporter when he lost his job. He had worked in construction and a lot of the construction was for different companies in Israel, and when they shut down the borders in response to some of Hamas's attacks, he lost his job, grew very bitter, and became an active member of Hamas.

Which part of Palestine were you living in?
J: I'd rather not say because there are still relatives there.

To further answer your question about the type of documents, when it came to businesses that employed me, it could be trade agreements between the various countries, because I could translate ten different languages and had verbal fluency in six of them. So when it came to Saudi Arabia or Iraq, I could translate most trade agreements for companies, so I generally worked freelance, going from place to place, and that was why my travel documents were so extensive.

When my husband became active in Hamas—and it was because he was unemployed and couldn't get a job anywhere else—he was involved in the kidnapping of some Israeli soldiers and the bombing of several synagogues in the area. Our town was a hotbed of Hamas activity known to the Israelis, so every time there would be a disruption of some kind, they would fire rockets into our village.

Would they bring tanks in?
J: They wouldn't bring tanks in because we were a little way away, and there was a lot of energy around us of anger against them, and they were afraid they would have to come in with a massive invasion force so as not to get cut off behind if they came in to our village. But it was not

so far that they couldn't send in rockets at us. This going back and forth went on for a number of months.

You did a daily trip to Israel and back?
J: During that period I was spending a lot of time just in Israel because I had a couple of freelance jobs for some corporations that were in negotiations. I was almost daily translating and checking documents for them, so I was communicating mainly by telephone with my family—my parents, siblings, and husband.

Then there was a massive attack by Hamas on a school and some buses. The Israeli government associated it with my village, and the whole night sky, as a survivor told me, was lit up with devices—bombs, incendiaries— that leveled two-thirds of our village. My husband, my parents, my grandmother, and all but one of my brothers were killed.

It was at that time, in my grief, that I was approached by Hamas. I was asked if I wanted to see that justice was done, and since I felt I had nothing to live for, nothing to go back to, I wanted to join my family, so I readily accepted their offer to be a human bomb, to take as many Israelis with me as I could. It was at that time, interestingly, that I was going to be doing some work for the government having to do with shipping contracts in Haifa, so it was decided that that was where I would become a martyr for the cause.

Thank you, Jasmin. Now I'll ask Ziv to introduce himself.
Z: I was a happy-go-lucky boy. I was one of—sort of what you might call "a mingler." Although I was born Palestinian, I spent a lot of time in Israel because my family was one of the few families allowed into Israel before all of—what we called "the cleansing" by them took place.

131

That was when they uprooted everyone of Palestinian lineage living in Israel and forced us out of the country.

Around this time, my father had had an accident in which his arm was injured, so that he was not able to work.

Was this a work-related accident?
Z: It was work-related; it had nothing to do with anything else. He had always been very religious and very ... quietly militant would be the best way to put it. He was not one who would stand on the street corner with stones, yelling at the Israeli tanks, but he would engage in the discussions in the coffeehouses about how we had to assert our rights. From the accident he had, he got an infection in his arm and became sicker and sicker. We were unable to get him the specialized treatment he needed because we would have had to get back into Israel and they would not allow us in.

Did you try to persuade them?
Z: My mother and father both tried everything and they would not let us in, so after a very painful eight months, my father passed away. My mother became even more bitter about things that were happening, and I began to get taken by her to these discussions that people were having. I saw them as our neighbors, but as it turned out, they were mostly Hamas people. They were talking about vengeance, about bringing Israelis to their knees, making them pay for everything they had done. My mother was almost rabid about how we had to get revenge for what had been done to my father, that *they* had allowed him to die. She had three children who were younger than me; I was the eldest, so she kept telling me how important it was for me to be the man of the family and to take care of the family business. I was very proud to have been given that honor.

How old were you at the time?

Z: I was eleven. I was a very carefree boy until that time, and then I felt the weight of destiny on my shoulders—at least I was made to believe the weight of destiny was on my shoulders. I was taken under the guidance of the Hamas leaders. They have special people who deal just with teens and pre-teens—recruiting them, inciting them, telling them the glory of giving their life for righteousness—and I believed that by blowing myself up and taking a bunch of non-believers with me, I would be doing the work of Allah.

So how did they recruit you?

Z: It was this gradual process of winning my confidence, building me up to these heights of being a person who could right wrong and create glorious vengeance for my father—whom I would then join in all of the glory.

How did you feel when they actually suggested that you become a bomber?

Z: By that time, after months and months of this indoctrination and telling me how great I was, it was put forth as my being a chosen one, and that it was a very big honor to be chosen.

How did your mother feel?

Z: My mother was all for it. As I said, she was almost rabid at this point—anything that would help get back at the Israelis for what had been done to her husband was worthwhile, so she was all for it. Then there was the fact that the Hamas leadership said that they would help provide for her and her other children if I were to do this, so I saw it also as the great reward that she was going to receive from this great honor that they had given me. I was completely deluded as to what the whole thing was about.

So the two of you got together at some point, did you?
Z: I didn't meet Jasmin until two days before we were to become bombers.

Had you gone into Israel by then?
Z: Yes, I had gone into Israel as the son of a businessman who did business in Israel. They had forged papers saying that I was his son, and they told the border guards that we were going to go to the beaches for a little vacation and that the rest of the family was going to join us there. We went to a rental house on the beach, and there was a whole large group of people there.

Jasmin and I were two of the martyrs, and we were treated lavishly—anything we wanted we could have, and we were constantly being told what a fantastically beautiful thing we were doing and what a change it was going to make.

There was one other person there who was going to be a martyr: a man about Jasmin's age, late 20s. He had been a "soldier" in the fight and had lost an eye and part of an arm. He played a beggar on the street, with signs written in Hebrew that said he was a war returnee—suggesting to those who give him money that he was Israeli, but of course he was not, and he was going to go down to a shopping mall and take up his position. Jasmin was to go into a nightclub area. On the beach, the nightclubs started early and went late. The early crowd would be the teenagers and the older people, and the evening crowd would be the twenty-somethings, so she was going to go in then. My position was the market where they sold food out of all the stalls, and you could hardly move when all the people were there.

Jasmin, did you feel they were deliberately trying to encourage your support of the violence, or were you giving the whole of yourself to it?

J: I was completely on board with it. I wanted vengeance. I wanted to see other families torn apart as my family had been torn apart, and as many of them as possible.

How did you feel about an 11-year-old boy being used?

J: I didn't see him as being used; I saw him as a willing volunteer, a disciple for the cause. I could identify with him and the hatred he felt for the Israelis because of their denying his father the help he needed.

Let us go to the day of the bombing. How were you given the bombs?

J: They had everything in the house on the beach where we were living. The bombs were made into—I guess you'd call it almost a corset for me. They were around my waist and chest area, with some additional ones on my back. Under loose-fitting clothes you couldn't see anything at all.

Were you dressed like an Israeli?

J: I was dressed like a tourist in flowing clothes. The nice thing about the area was not only were there Israelis, but there were a lot of tourists from other countries and people coming off the cruise ships. It was an area where nobody questioned anything you had on as long as it looked summery. If you were to go out there in a black coat, they might question you.

Ziv, how were you strapped in?

Z: I had a backpack. Because I had a very slight body, they were able only to put a row of bombs around my waist, and they decided that wasn't enough to cause major damage, so I also had a backpack on that was wired in synchronization with the bombs. I had a device in my pocket, and all I had to do was reach in and push it and everything would explode.

Back to you, Jasmin. Tell us what happened.
J: I went into one of the very popular restaurant-cum-cafés. They had an area where you could sit down and be served, and they also had an area where you could buy sandwiches because a lot of people bought things and took them out to the beach and the deck. So I went to the back and stood in line among a throng of people. It was a very busy time, early afternoon—past what you would consider lunch but the starting time for a lot of people. I got in line and held back a little bit because there weren't quite enough people when I first got there. There was a refrigerated case of drinks and salads and things next to me, and I pretended to be looking at what was there and couldn't make up my mind—until more and more people came in. When I felt people press up against me, I said to my husband and my parents, "I'm coming to see you," and I pressed the button.

What happened then?
J: There was a flash of light, and I had no sense of anything physical.

No pain?
J: No pain. I was just immediately completely surrounded in light. I had closed my eyes as I pressed the button. I opened them, and there was my family. They were all there, and they came and welcomed me. It was a feeling of the weight of the world being lifted off me—that everything was all right, that everything I had been so sad about, that had torn me apart for the many months before this incident, was completely gone.

And what happened to you, Ziv?

Z: I was about two blocks away from where Jasmin was. I heard her explosion go off, and for some reason I was drawn to it. I had only gone about half a block when people started running toward me. They had pieces of glass in their faces, and there was blood dripping down; there was a man missing a hand; there was a little child crying. For the first time, I realized that what they meant by revenge was causing the same agony to other people that I had felt when my father died, and it just didn't seem like my place to be the cause of this. Then I was very aware of the weight of the bombs on my back and the constriction of the belt around my waist, and I didn't want to hurt anybody. I just didn't want to hurt anybody.

What did you do?

Z: There were sirens and people running all over. I saw an Israeli soldier directing traffic, and I walked up to him and told him, "I have a bomb on me, and I'm supposed to set it off, but I don't want to." He said something into the walkie-talkie he had with him, and immediately there were about a dozen people around me and they were clearing everybody away from me. Then some men in suits that were all padded came, and they surrounded me. There was an area they had set up that had these big iron sheets around it, and they told me to come with them. I was getting very frightened. I thought maybe they would kill me, but they seemed very nice. I gave them the detonator, the thing I had in my pocket, but it was connected to wires, so somebody beside me in one of the stuffed suits was holding it as we walked toward this enclosed area. Then the world went dark.

What happened?

137

Z: As I looked down, I could see my body on the street, and my head was practically gone. I then played it back, and I remembered hearing a gun go off and something hitting me right behind my right ear. I looked down, and all of the people who were around me were looking back over behind me and to the right with their guns raised, trying to find where the shot had come from. I then went into brightness, into light, and my father came, and I was very confused.

Did he explain what had happened?
J: I asked him—I said, "What happened? I was trying to help them." And he said—he used to call me Poopi—he said, "Poopi, it wasn't them; it was Hamas. They didn't want you to tell where they were or identify who they were." And he told me that he was very proud of me because I had made my own choice.

We have now, here, two situations: somebody who has let off a bomb and somebody who has deliberately not let off a bomb. Jasmin, how do you evaluate your action now that you're on the Other Side?
J: I see it as part of the third-dimensional judgment of saying that there are things that are very definitely right and things that are very definitely wrong, of saying that there has to be a response for every action that occurs. If I am injured, harmed, or have my property taken, that gives me the right to injure, harm, or take the property of others.

You don't believe that now?
J: I don't believe in that at all. I believe that concept, that mentality, is a reason why we souls go to Earth, so that we may experience it and make choices within that framework. Now I see that that is nothing more than lessons where we allow ourselves to make choices.

So do you judge yourself for doing the wrong thing?
J: Oh, absolutely not.

Why? You've just told me it was the wrong thing.
J: It was not the wrong thing; it was the lesson I was working on in that lifetime, to understand what revenge was all about, what anger was about, what hatred was about, what I thought power was about, and then to come Home and realize it wasn't power at all.

You took on hatred for yourself. You took on total power over other people by being able to annihilate them. Isn't that a cause for regret?
J: There is no regret at Home. Everything that we do on Earth is to learn lessons. If we souls do not experience the extremes of emotions, we do not fully understand them. It isn't until we get to the point of being so invested and absorbed in the emotions of, say, hatred or revenge that we can truly feel the dynamic effect that it can have on a human psyche.

So you're all the wiser for this?
J: Absolutely. I know it's something I do not need to experience again. I would be able to advise a soul now, if it chose to do something like that, what it might be facing, but to me it is nothing more than a lesson like what it was like to have a romantic relationship with my husband.

Ziv, I suppose you're congratulating yourself because you did the right thing.
Z: I don't see it as the "right thing." I see it, as Jasmin has said, as a learning experience, a lesson. My lesson was having enough confidence in myself to know that I had a choice. It wasn't about did I blow people up or did I not blow people up. It was about who has the ability or the power to control what I do, and the answer is I do, myself.

That was what I learned. My whole lesson was about confidence in myself and realizing that I was as important as they were. My decisions, my feelings, were as important as anybody else's, and I had the ability to change the pattern that had been set in motion.

Aren't you angry that you were killed so young?
Z: No, because my lesson was to learn that I could do that, and once I learned that a soul has total control of itself, the lessons I went to Earth for were complete.

Ziv, what are you doing now?
Z: I'm just about ready to come back. I have chosen this time a musical career because I want to learn something about the effect that music can have on soothing the body.

What part of the world will you be in?
Z: I haven't totally decided yet. It's between Argentina and Japan, because they each have totally different ways of looking at music.

And Jasmin, what are you doing now?
J: Right now I am still integrating the various lessons I learned in my time on Earth. I don't feel that I have truly appreciated all of the little consequences of actions that we take on Earth, and that was one of the reasons I had gone there, so I'm still in debriefing.

Is it a difficult time for you?
J: No, it's a very interesting time, a very informative time.

Are you getting help?
J: Oh, absolutely—my council is working with me, and several others who had experienced some of the same things that I did.

One last question: why did your guides not talk you out of it?

J: Because that's not what guides are for. Guides are to be there if we ask them a question about which they can give us some guidance, but guidance does not mean taking us by the hand and leading us. They cannot affect us in any way that would interfere with our exercising our freedom of choice.

Jasmin, Ziv, thank you very much for telling us how you died.

How I Died (and what I did next)

Earthquake

Amita, can you please tell us about your life before the earthquake?
I was born in the area around Kashmir. My family herded animals. I was the eldest daughter in the family—seven children were born and four of us lived past the age of three.

When in Earth time was this?
I was born in your late 1980s. We were very poor, so as soon as it became possible, we children would go out and do work to help support the family. I started working for a weaver when I was thirteen. We took local materials from the shepherds and wove them into cloth. The place where I worked was a large, long building where we had the different processing areas for the materials as they came in. At first I was in the sorting department—there were sticks and little rocks and things that had become mixed in with the materials, and I would feel through them and pull those out before the wool was put into the separators and spinners.

It was very hard work, and it was a 12-hour day. Basically we worked six days a week—they'd say we worked six days, but sometimes we worked seven because they liked to rotate the day off. But it brought in a little money for the family. As I said, when I began working I did the sorting. Then, as I got older and my hands got stronger from pulling the wool apart, I went into the area that separated the wool and started working spinning it into thread. I did that for longer than a year and then went into the dying department where we put colors onto the wool.

What sort of materials did you use for dying?
They came in powder form. They said most of them were from the local area, from minerals and things that they had ground up. I don't know exactly what they all were. It wasn't important for any of us to be educated in how things worked. It was just important for us to work to provide money. My brothers did get some schooling, but I never went to a school because it wasn't important for women to do anything other than work, provide for the family, and maybe be a mother and provide more hands to work.

What religion were you?
Primarily the family was Muslim. I say primarily because I never really had a chance to go and study anything about the religion. I was told our religion says we will do this or that, we will eat this or we will eat that, we will honor the deity at a certain time—and I just went through the motions of whatever I was told to do.

After I became about 17 and my body was bigger, I got to go into the weaving room. The weaving room was better because that was the one place where you actually got to sit part of the time. You weren't standing for 12 hours or pulling for 12 hours or bending over for 12 hours. But it took a lot of care to watch and make sure that you had all the colors in the right place. They would have a picture, and you would have to line up the colors according to the picture and then make sure that there was always thread of the right color for each one of the positions, and that the spools were changed when they needed to be changed, and that the—they called it a shuttle—that the shuttle was going back and forth correctly and didn't become entangled.

This was a mechanical loom?
It was partially mechanical, but it worked a lot on foot power: you had to press your feet up and down to get it to move back and forth. I worked with the shuttles almost two years.

For my entire life we had had tremors, but just before the time I was to go back home, it was almost like the Earth wanted to tremble, and it would start, but something would stop it. It was like a resistance, like I found when the threads weren't moving correctly—I could just feel this energy of a resistance. The other girls and I talked about how that wasn't a good sign because the energy wasn't able to go where it wanted to go, but we didn't know what that meant. Then one day everything just broke loose. The Earth started trembling and it just went on trembling, and as it did, the first things I noticed were cracks in the walls. The walls began to crack, and then the ceiling fell in because the walls couldn't support it any longer.

Didn't you run out of the building?
It happened so fast that, as the quake began, I fell off my stool, and as I fell, my leg became tangled in the lower part of the machine and I couldn't get it out before the roof came down. I was hearing all of the other women and girls screaming and crying out, and then I heard this terrible rumbling—the hillside not far from us was coming our way. As the wall started coming toward me and I saw these huge boulders, I knew that I was going to be buried. I didn't want to die slowly and be buried alive, so I just said to Allah, "I want to come with you now," and I left my body.

145

I was able to go above the rubble and I watched the rest of the hillside come down, completely cover the building where we had been, and continue on another good distance before it stopped. As I looked out over the area, I saw that entire section of the city was completely transformed. You couldn't see that human beings had ever been there. It was like it had been erased and completely covered with a new section of the Earth.

At that point, my three little siblings, who had passed on as well, came running to me and hugged me. Even though they were three or younger when they passed on, they knew me and welcomed me because, being the eldest, I had taken care of them. My grandmother came, too, and a couple of my aunts, and it was a joyful reunion.

Where were you when this reunion took place?
I was in a brightly lit area that was very, very beautiful. The rubble was nowhere to be seen. If I looked down to the place where my feet were, it was as if I was on a cloud. It was very peaceful. There was no sensation of pain where the machine had caught my foot; my foot had hurt until I asked for Allah to take me, after which I had no pain whatsoever.

Was Allah there?
No, because as I now know, we are all part of Source, and the entity known to my then religion as Allah is a part of all of us, and we of him. The energy was there, but a specific divine energy was not, just the energy of the universe which is contained in all of us.

What have you done since the earthquake?
First I worked with my advisors and those people who had met me to help me fully comprehend what had happened and who I was. I was in a kind of a daze when I first went

across. I understood where I was, but I still had all the urgent feelings of a desire to take care of those who were in my earthly home—that I had to provide money, and that I had to make sure my sister and two brothers who were still there were taken care of.

But you couldn't.
I couldn't, but I had the urge, so I had to be re-acclimated to the fact that, as a soul, that was just a part I had been playing to learn lessons about existing in poverty and giving of myself. I had to be able to discipline myself to understand the choices I had made to put myself there in the first place.

And so, having done that work on yourself, have you been involved in any specific activity on the Other Side?
Once I fully remembered who I was, I was able to help others who came back with confusion and the energy of some of their belief systems from their physical form to understand that those things still require a judgment, a sense of right and wrong, whereas now as souls, we simply use our experiences to evaluate the new knowledge we obtained so that we have the wisdom of it and don't have to do it again.

So are you planning to come back to Earth again?
Not in the foreseeable future. I am very much enjoying helping those who come through to understand what they are doing. I am becoming a teacher, possibly because in that life I was never allowed to even be a student.

Thank you, Amita, for telling us how you died.

How I Died (and what I did next)

Suicide

Toshi, you lived in Japan. Tell me about your life there.
My life was one spent in my family. We lived together with
many generations: my mother and father, of course; my
grand-parents; there was my aunt with her two boys; and
myself.

Were you poor or wealthy or somewhere in the middle?
Somewhere in the middle. My parents were the first to be
able to really get a good education. My grandfather was a
farmer who moved to the city to try to have a regular
income. My grandmother still worked very, very hard. My
grandfather had passed on. This is on my mother's side. On
my father's side, they still lived out in the countryside.

What part of Japan did you come from?
Our home place was in central Japan, very near to
Nagasaki, and our family had moved into Nagasaki.

As you tell the story, tell me how you remember yourself.
I was just entering my teen years—I was eleven.

And what was going on in your life?
My life was one of constant pressure to excel. My father
and mother were the first in their families to be able to go
on to higher education, and it afforded them an
opportunity to get into sort of a middle-management level,
as they kept saying. They were telling me that I was going
to be the first one in the family to become a president of a

149

corporation. Everything surrounding my life was learning, learning, learning, learning—education from morning till night—what have you learned, how are you doing?

And no sports?
No sports. There was exercise, because that was very important. There would be the morning exercise, even at the school I went to; we started each morning with calisthenics.

You must have been glad to be with your schoolmates.
Well, the school I went to was one for excelling. It was not a place where you developed friendships; it was a place where you tried to be better than everybody else, so you didn't trust anyone. It was constant competition; even from the age of four or five years, when I started learning in the pre-school, it was always: Who's the best in the class? Who knows the most? Who has begun to do writing? Everything was based on competition.

Didn't you have any friends in your spare time?
I didn't have any spare time. Every moment was learning something. If it wasn't regular school subjects, my parents would have something, as they called it, "for enrichment." It would be an encyclopedia; it would be a history of another land; it would be the beginning of learning languages. It was all constantly how much can you cram into your head? I felt that there was a funnel being put into my ear, and everything was constantly being dripped inside.

Is the rest of the country not as programmed as this school?
There were some other schools like this, but the majority—while they were very concerned with making

sure you were well-rounded and educated—didn't go to the extreme that the school my parents found for me did.

What were the teachers like?
The teachers were like little warlords. They would stand over you with a bamboo rod, and if you got a wrong answer, you would get your knuckles slapped. If you didn't have all of your homework done, if you couldn't answer a question, you would get rapped.

Were there worse punishments than that?
If you were caught—what they considered—cheating, even your eyes wandering during an exam, you would get three to seven on the behind, depending upon how egregious they thought it was. If you were actually caught taking somebody else's information during an exam, you were expelled, and once expelled, it was total humiliation for you and your entire family.

Were there many kids who opted out by getting expelled?
There were some who just couldn't stand the pressure, and they found that an easy way to get out of the pressure, because their parents were as insistent as mine. Mine thought this education was the only way that I was going to be able to fulfill the dreams they had for me.

Did you have doubts about that?
At first, no. At first, this was what I had been taught; this was what the world was about; this was the way I was supposed to go; this was my destiny. As I was told on numerous occasions, particularly by my grandmother: "This is your destiny; you are meant to be the great person in our family," and I saw it at first as truly being what I was supposed to be. In the beginning, I didn't have any trouble

keeping up because it was rather easy to just have six or seven subjects to take care of, but as I got older and they began having an average of ten subjects in each period, I found that I didn't have the time to learn everything.

It wasn't a question of brain power, but oft packing it all in?
It was a question of having the time to be able to physically read the material. And you could read the material, but for me, in order to understand it, I had to sit and think about it.

So how did you feel about that?
I began to get disillusioned as to whether this was really my destiny. If it was my destiny, why was it almost impossible for me to find the time to do it? I didn't play; I didn't have any video games like the kids I saw in the neighborhood; I didn't have anything but my books. Every birthday and holiday, the presents were more books. They were never video games or balls or anything like that, because that would take time away from the study.

So you had no childhood.
Now, knowing what childhood is, I would say no. At that time I didn't know what I was missing. I just saw that the others were wasting time, as my family said. One of the additional problems within the family concerned my cousins. Both of them had what you would call a photographic memory. They could take a look at something and they would remember it. I had to work to remember something. So when my parents compared me with my cousins, I looked like I was not putting the effort into it because it came so easily to them.

Were they in the same school?

They were in the same school, and of course, we were in the same household. They would make fun of me when it took me a while to catch on to a concept, though I understood things at a deeper level than they did because they could just parrot back to you what they had read without understanding it. One cousin was a year older than I and the other a year younger, and even the younger one seemed to excel beyond what I was able to do even with my greater effort. They did have time to play because it took them no time at all to do their daily assignments.

Making a judgment about your mental powers, were you, in fact, working to capacity?
I was working as hard as I possibly could, every spare moment, because I wanted to please my parents and my whole family. I wanted to fulfill the dreams that they kept telling me their whole life was based upon—their whole life was based upon my reaching a level that they only dreamed as a possibility.

So your work was really for their sake rather than your own.
As I look at it now, it was totally for their sake. I was not enjoying what I was doing. Most of the subjects they directed me toward were things I had no interest in. I was interested in the printed word, literature, and social studies, but they kept directing me toward mathematics and science, and while I had a slight interest in them, it was not to the degree that they wished me to have. In the beginning, I also had difficulty with other languages because there was no one to practice with, since no one in the household spoke the languages. My cousins were taking totally different things; they were completely enmeshed in science. They weren't being pushed as much

toward languages as I was, and I had nobody to communicate with except at school.

You've given us a picture of the real frustration you had. How did you answer that frustration?
For a number of years I just kept plodding along. I would put my head down, jump into everything I did, take every waking moment, and it got to the point where my anxiety was getting so high that I wasn't sleeping. I was spending all my time working, thinking if I took one more hour, I'd be able to get it; another hour and I'd be a master of it. But it just kept happening—I'd put the time in and the time in and the time in, and I couldn't catch up. I seemed always to be a day or two behind where I was supposed to be. And then I began to do poorly on some of the exams from lack of having the time to get to the subject matter. I would spend time to understand something, and when I looked at the clock, it was time to go to bed and I hadn't gotten to the other subjects.

What was the way out?
The way out for me, I thought, was to talk to my parents and let them know that I had the capability to be a good student and gain admission to good schools, but I could not do it the way they wanted me to do it. I had to do it at a little slower pace. I was not like my cousins; I could not grasp things as rapidly as they did. For about 18 months I argued back and forth with my parents that I needed to go to a less intense school. They saw that as a total failure on their part to motivate me properly. I saw it as a complete mis-understanding of my abilities, and we seemed to be at a huge impasse. They were getting frustrated. They were screaming at me that I was worthless, I was no son of theirs because I couldn't do this. My cousins made fun of

me. I was an outcast in my own family, and it was at that time that I thought the only thing I could do was just leave.

Run away?
Well, I thought first of running away, but at my age I had no way to support myself. I was aware of what they called urchins who lived on the street, some of the kids who had been thrown out of their families or whose families had disintegrated, and I saw them as being even more miserable than I, so it was at that time that I decided the easiest way would be to kill myself—to step out and end it all. I was in constant misery. I felt totally alone. My family was all against me. I was continually in trouble at school because I wouldn't have all of my work done. It just seemed as if nobody cared about me, and I did feel the traditional pressure of being a total failure and dishonoring not only myself but my family, and I couldn't live with that dishonor.

So what did you do?
Not too far from our house was a hillside that looked over an industrial area, which had been cut into the hillside for more space. It was fenced off and quite protected, but there was a way to get under the fence. There was a steep drop-off from there that went down onto railroad tracks. One night, after everybody had gone to bed while I was still working (which was standard—everybody would go to bed and I would still be up working), I decided that I just couldn't take it anymore. So I left a brief note for my parents that simply said "For the honor of the family" and snuck out. I took the couple of awards I had received when I had first started school, before it became too unbearable, and pinned them on my shirt to let people know I was not a total failure. Then I went out and jumped off the cliff.

155

And what happened when you jumped off the cliff?
I felt myself floating, and it was the first time I felt free. I didn't feel burdened by anything. Then there was a light, and beautiful vapors, I would call them, came and surrounded me, and I felt loved—possibly for the first time in maybe seven or eight years. I felt loved; I felt that I was important.

Who was telling you that?
It turned out they were my guides. They had been with me, but I hadn't opened myself to listen to them because I was so busy concentrating on what I thought was important.

Were you aware of what happened to your body and afterward?
I did look down and see it crumbled. I had fallen into a transportation area where there were railroad tracks and storage cars and things like that, and it just looked like a bundle of rags that had been tossed away.

Was that all, or did you go to the funeral?
No, I didn't feel that I had a connection any longer to my Earthly family. I felt that it had been a lesson for them on using another human to try to create something that they themselves could never accomplish. For me it was that I had to realize my limitations, and I had realized them. My lesson was also to understand that I did have some choice, and my choice was not to live as a slave to their dreams.

Were you criticized on the Other Side for taking your own life?
Oh, absolutely not, because it was part of the lessons; it was my realization that I had a choice. Considering the physical setup on Earth, had I remained, I would not have had any choices. I would have continually been in a

situation where I was dominated by what was expected of me, not by any choices that I made. Once I realized I had a choice, had some power over myself, the only way I could get out of that situation was to return Home.

So after you were met by your spirit guides, what happened to you next?
I went back and gradually began remembering some of those souls who came up to me. It was very interesting because I remembered what friendship was; I remembered what love was; I remembered what having fun was all about. That was something that had been totally put aside for those 11 years. I again realized that these are all lessons that we put ourselves through so that we can learn more about ourselves. The freedom of being at Home, the joy of sharing unconditional love with people, was so much sweeter than it had felt before, because I had known what it was to be without it.

Do they ask you to study and work on the Other Side?
No. On the Other Side it's completely what you want to do. Not that you can't sit and be what you call a couch potato—you can if you want to; you can just sit and watch the world go by if you want to. (Not that we sit—we actually float because we don't have bodies.) But you decide what you want to do. If you want to study something, you study it. If you want to observe something, you observe it. If you want to take advantage of the knowledge that somebody else had gotten, you suck in the knowledge, see how it feels, and see if you have an application for it.

Can you also observe what is happening on Earth?
If you put your consciousness in that direction, yes.

But you haven't chosen to.
No. I don't feel a connection to the physical part of myself that was.

Are you really burned out with all you've been through?
Not as soon as I got Home—that was like taking off old, dirty clothes and disposing of them and getting attired in a fresh, new suit that buoyed my spirit.

By the sound of it, you don't want to come back to another life.
Not for a while. I want to observe more, and when I come back, I guarantee it will not be into a pressure cooker.

Thank you so much, Toshi, for telling us how you died.

Family Honor

Tell me what you'd like to say, Jairaj.
J: When in body form, I was from a very high family within Indian society, and there were great expectations placed upon me.

Which caste were you in?
J: It was what we called the "government caste" because everyone went into government service. The type of service we went into, or the particular division, depended upon our education and the influence of our families. I was the eldest son of three, and I was always the one in whom everybody put their hopes that I could go into management government, into the higher echelons, after I did my time of service. For this reason, I was sent to all of the best universities. I had training at Oxford, and I also did a master's degree at Harvard in the U.S. This was all in international relations and social politics. While I was finishing up my advanced degree at Harvard, my family made an agreement for marriage for me so that my betrothed and I would have a family and could open our house to politicians, business people, and government people to advance my career.

Had you met Solita before?
J: No, not before I came back from the U.S. I found her to be absolutely captivating. She was just beautiful. She was like a precious flower. I saw her as a lotus that I could bow down to and absorb into my very being. There was an

immediate connection between us, and for once, I was glad that my parents had done all of the research to get somebody who was so absolutely beautiful for me.

Solita, how did you feel about this marriage?
S: At first I was a little concerned because I had always been a romantic and wanted to marry for love, but when I first saw Jairaj, there was an immediate connection with us. On our first accompanied date, we laughed during the entire meal, and I knew at that time that this was somebody with whom I could share my life.

Was there much of an age difference between you?
S: Jairaj was eight years older. I was just 22 and he was 30, but that is not unusual in our community.

Had you, as souls, worked together in another life?
S: Yes, we are actually soul mates, so we had been together in many different lives. Of course, we had no memory of that, but it was one of the things that made our mating during this life a very easy and comfortable thing.

What happened next?
J: Once I returned from the United States I began as a junior diplomat. One of my assignments was to be a liaison with the U.S. embassy to help them deal with all the local restrictions, registrations, licensing, and everything that affected U.S. citizens who had come to India. I found the work to be extremely tedious—not so much from the American standpoint, because they were almost nonchalant about things, but because of my government, which wanted to make sure that everything was exactly as they wanted it to be and that they were not being taken advantage of.

Indian bureaucracy is very powerful, I believe.
J: It is extremely powerful, and your immediate supervisors and your supervisors' supervisors let you know that you are constantly being monitored, constantly watched, and that your very life within your career depends upon every moment of every day. The pressure was tremendous.

You're giving me the feeling that you were regretting what you had chosen as a career.
J: I was beginning to regret it. I was beginning to realize, particularly as my marriage unfolded and there was such joy and love at home, that I had to drag myself away from bliss and submit myself to torture.

Did you have depression as one of your characteristics?
J: Prior to the employment, no, but I did start to have all of the major symptoms of depression within a year of my employment. The time frame on this was: I came back from the U.S., and within a matter of six months, Solita and I were wed, because the family felt that with my age and the fact that I was entering into this high position, I needed to have an established family immediately. During the six-month period I was in training for what they called the diplomacy end of what my job would be. I was not actually attached to any specific job, but I was being indoctrinated in all of the various pathways that things had to traverse in order to get opinions from the government and from the higher agencies. It was like a continuation of my schooling, but a schooling solely in bureaucracy. It was during this period of time that I saw the human angle that was becoming so powerful for me at home was being stripped from me within the workplace.

161

You almost had a schizophrenic situation.
J: I felt like two people. I was the delighted bridegroom at home, and I was the harried, unseen worker at the office.

Was your attitude harming your progress?
J: I don't quite understand your question.

Well, you seem to have been depressed and annoyed by the work that you were coming into. Did that inhibit your progress?
J: Progress didn't really begin until the assignment with the embassy began, and then when I had the pleasure of working with the Americans, I got back into the same relaxed atmosphere that I had had when I studied in the U.S. Not that my studies allowed me to relax, but those people knew how to relax and I enjoyed that. But then when I would have to carry through the second half of my work, which was dealing with the Indian government, I met nothing but frustration. I kept asking them: Look, I am Indian, I am your emissary here. Why are you fighting everything that I try to do? I'm only seeking information so that I may convey it to the Americans so that they will comply with what you want. Why are you making it so difficult for them and, therefore, also for me?

Solita, were you conscious of the difficulties your husband was going through?
S: Jairaj never talked about work at home, but when he would return at the end of the day, it was as if a ghost had walked through the door. It would be a shell that had this pallor and this great cloud around it, but within a matter of less than an hour he would be his old self again. He would be the person who courted me, and we would enjoy our time together. He generally worked six days a week, but on the day that he had off, we would just spend time together

and take walks through a variety of gardens and visit the temples, and it was like I had a happy little boy with me who was released from all of the stresses of his life.

When did this situation change in a negative way, Jairaj?
J: The point at which I realized things were not going right was at my first six-month evaluation within the government agency. I was told at that time that they were not happy with my attitude, that they thought I was too Westernized. Then at the one-year evaluation, they told me that they had not seen any progress during the previous six months, and that if I continued they would have to put me on probation, and if that did not work they would terminate me. At my 18-month evaluation they put me on probation, and the reasons they gave me were that I did not seem to be working for the Indian government, but I seemed to be holding myself apart from them, so they did not feel that I was a team player. It was at this time that they began to hint that not only would I be terminated, but I would not be able to get any type of a job within the government agencies. I knew at that time that were my family to see me go through such a thing, it would absolutely crush them. I had my youngest brother just about to enter government service, and I feared that if I were dismissed, it would have an effect also upon the way he was regarded, and I began to worry that I was going to destroy my family.

Was there any way in which you could change from the situation you were in to a different one within the government?
J: With each evaluation I asked about that. I asked them to put me into something that would be more structured so that I could get a sense of what it was they wanted me to

163

do. They said they would think about it, but then they would say that I was the only one currently available who had the credentials of an American degree, which was accepted by the Americans. Anyone else they would put into that position would not be so easily able to deal with the situation. That created such a conflict in my mind: If I was the only one who could do it, and I was doing such a good job, why was I getting such poor evaluations?

Did you find an answer to that question?
J: I never found an answer to that question. It began to be a situation where I developed a nervous affliction. I had chronic intestinal problems from nerves. I would get intense headaches when a deadline for something was coming up or a particular meeting with the ministry was set up. I was just falling apart physically.

Did you have bad health in your family history?
J: No, our family had always been extremely strong, and I had always been extremely strong. When other people around me would get ill with viruses, it would never affect me.

So this was a question of the family honor, whether or not you could live up to the situation.
J: It was more that than anything else. It was my parents; it was the lineage within the family; it was a legacy for my brothers; and it was a face for my beloved, how she was perceived, how we were perceived.

In that last probationary time, Solita, how was your husband?
S: It was interesting because Jairaj never told me about the evaluations. I noticed that periodically he would become more depressed or more withdrawn, but only as he came

home. There was like a transformation that took place once he got home, but it was beginning to take longer and longer for that transformation from the harried worker into the loving husband.

Did you have children by that time?
S: No, we were not blessed with children.

So, Jairaj, how did this come to a head?
J: It came to a head when I realized that I was going to be terminated and that my worst fears about the intense impact on my family would materialize. I came up with a plan at that time that if there were to be an accident in which I was killed, my family would not be perceived as having a failure amongst them. It would just be that there was an accident. There are notoriously bad drivers in India, so I figured they would not question anything were I to have an accident. Then I began to believe that Solita, who was so close to me, would not be able to survive without me. I also did not want her to be put back into a situation where she would just be bartered away to someone else, so it became clear to me that I also had to take her with me.

You saw this as an act of love?
J: I saw taking her with me as an act of love. I saw getting rid of myself as a matter of honor within the family.

So what happened?
J: Shortly before the final evaluation, which was when I knew I would be terminated, I put in for holiday time, and Solita and I started planning a trip to visit distant relatives of hers in other locations. We got everything ready for the trip. I was sure that I could very easily allow myself to die,

but I didn't know whether she would be able to or not. My plan was to take the car and drive it into a water retention area and let the car sink and have us both drown. I was firm in my belief that I would stay there, but I didn't want her to go on, so my plan was to give her a sleeping draught in a cup of tea so that she would be asleep when I went off the road.

So we planned our holiday and got all ready to go; I filled up a container with tea, which we had the practice of always taking with us, and we began our trip. When we were in an area where I knew there was a retention pond, I stopped for a rest, saying the call of nature was imminent for me, and when I came back I said, "Let's have a cup of tea and some biscuits before we go on." I took her cup and put some powder in it, and we sat and had just the most lovely conversation. We talked about the future, because she had no idea what was coming, and I talked about how I felt so much better, that I knew I could conquer my physical problems, that it was all a matter of my mind allowing me to create these disabilities. We got back in the car and a very short while later she was snoozing. I knew she was in a very deep sleep because I tried to awaken her. I then approached the area; there was a drop-off into the retention pond, and I put the vehicle into gear, pressed on the accelerator, and held her in my arms as the car went over.

And what happened after that?
J: After that, I know the point where I left my body, and I know the point where Solita left her body, because I saw her spirit go, but I had trouble following her. It was like I was in a maze. It was a maze of confusion, a maze of...should I have done this...what if I had done this...and I seemed to just be in that place for an infinitely long period of time.

Let's return to that in a minute. Solita, were you aware of leaving your body and what had happened to it?
S: It was interesting, because Jairaj was so loving as we stopped at the rest stop, and we laughed as we enjoyed the tea and biscuits, but there seemed to be such a sadness within his eyes. I commented on it and he said no, it was only that we seemed to be moving from one part of our life into another part of our life, and then he told me how positive he was that things were going to change for the better.

The next thing I was aware of was looking down on my body submerged in a car. As soon as the realization hit me that my body was in a car under water, I knew that I had passed over, and my blessed aunt, who was always my confidant as I was growing up and who had passed away some five years previously, came out of a tunnel of light and welcomed me. I felt the intense, unconditional love that was all around me, and it was absolutely beautiful. I said to her, "I have to go back—I have to help Jairaj," and she told me that he was on his own pathway and that when he was ready he would join us.

Did you realize what had happened?
S: I didn't realize that he had given me a draught to make me sleep. I did realize that the car had gone off the road and that we had drowned in the water. The whole sequence of events I had no idea about.

So, Jairaj, you didn't have her help. You were confused.
J: I was confused because I was second-thinking everything that had happened in the previous three years—my time in the States, my training, my marriage, my various evaluations, my performance, my decision to bring her with me as I transitioned—and I had such guilt that I was

preventing her from enjoying a full life. I was wandering around in self-pity, regret, anger, a total sense of worthlessness.

Did you have the feeling that you were in the place where you died, or had you gone back to your family home?
J: It varied. As I would fixate on one particular thing, it was as if I were there but not able to be seen. When I thought about the decisions I had made while in school, I was in school seeing the decisions, seeing the options. When I applied for government service, I saw the application and how if I had answered it differently I might have been assigned a different position. But I had wanted to maintain an international connection, something that, when I wanted to run for political office, would make me look as if I had my finger on the pulse of everything that was going on. When I thought about the evaluations, I went into the thinking of the people; for a time I was able to understand why they were perceiving what they were perceiving, but it was an erroneous perception.

Were you angry?
J: There was a lot of anger, and the angrier I got, the more I wanted to stay, the more I wanted to explain myself.

But you couldn't explain yourself because no one would hear you.
J: Nobody could hear me, nobody could see me. I had taken care of that.

Were you aware of what happened to your bodies?
J: It was never an issue. My whole time was being played out in thought. The body was the last thing that I thought about, the least thing that had any pull or pressure on me.

How long did this process take?

J: In Earth time it took in excess of four months.

And then?
J: Then one day it was as if I realized: I can't do anything about this because I carried my plan out—I have withdrawn myself from the physical. When I opened to that idea, I heard Solita calling, and she said, "Jairaj, I'm waiting for you." Then I knew that what I had been occupying myself with had nothing to do with who I was. For the first time I realized that I wasn't just Jairaj, that that was just one instance of experience that I had, that I was a soul and that the soul that had been Solita was a very dear friend of mine and could help me to understand everything that had happened.

Did people blame you for committing murder and suicide?
J: No, at Home nobody blames you. They just inquire if you've learned what you needed to from the experience.

Have you?
J: I have learned most of the lessons. My council has been very beneficial in that regard, as has the soul I knew as Solita, and others. It took releasing the physical energies, the physical emotions, so that I could step back from them and see the effect they had upon me and upon others, to make me be able to evaluate what the wisdom was within the actions.

And finally, Solita, did you learn lessons?
S: I learned a number of lessons, but most of them were earlier in my life before I was married. They had to do primarily with patience and issues of wanting to control. A little of that came into my marriage. But I did not have a lot of difficult lessons planned for that lifetime.

Had you made a contract with Jairaj?

169

S: Oh, absolutely, it was a contract, and it was a contract that it would be a short life for me, and that was why I had not planned so many difficult lessons. It was more for me to be a helpmate in letting Jairaj experience lessons that he needed or wanted than it was for me to experience individual lessons.

Jairaj and Solita, thank you for telling us how you died.

Starvation

Tell us a little bit about yourself, please, Ayana.
Before I transitioned I had reached 14 what you call years of age. We call them seasons—14 winter seasons.

This was in east Africa?
In Ethiopia. My parents were farmers, and from the time that I was about 12 seasons, the weather turned very bad. It got drier and drier.

What sort of farming did your parents do?
They did mostly grains—wheat and things of that nature—some maize. They had given up on root vegetables several years before because there was not enough ground water.

How did they till the land?
They tilled the land by hand, and occasionally, when there would be a time when the land had to be broken up, my father would hire one of the local men who had an animal that he could pull his hand plow behind for additional leverage.

What animal?
Water buffalo.

They're very strong, I believe.
Yes.

Tell me more.

171

We were a large family—originally there were eight of us children. I was the eldest. My mother seemed always to be ready for another one. When the weather began getting bad and all of us were eating less and less, as my mother had the babies, it seemed that there was something wrong with them. By the time I was eleven, two sisters and a brother had died, so there were then just five of us children. My mother's health was very, very poor. There was a midwife in the area for her deliveries, but there were no big doctors or anything around.

What sort of house did you live in?
It was the usual for the area, made of mud bricks and thatch.

Was it a round house?
More or less round. I think my father had a little bit of difficulty with creating angles. He and his brothers, my uncles, built the house.

Did it have windows, or was it completely enclosed?
It had ventilation up toward the top, which allowed in a little light. It didn't have windows that we could look out, but you could look out the door. We didn't spend much time inside except for the few times that it rained hard, and at night to sleep.

Where did you sleep?
We slept on beds of hay that were fresh—when we had it. We had some thin blankets and animal skins that we also used for beds.

It got cold at night, did it?
It got rather chilly so we would pile on whatever we had, and we generally slept in a communal bed for warmth.

It must have been difficult dealing with the extremes of heat and cold.

You got used to it; from as far as I could remember, it just was. There wasn't a whole lot of change in my childhood. There were the rainy seasons we could look forward to, which gave some break, and the temperatures were more moderate or within a closer range during those periods of time, but when the heat began, when what you call the drought began, then it was just hot and it seemed to get hotter.

Had your family lived on the land in that part of Ethiopia for long?

Four generations they could go back, from the tribal times when they first started tilling the land, but for three generations—my father from his father and his father— each generation had acquired larger and larger sections of land. At the time I was born it was almost more than my father could do by himself. My uncles, his brothers, were very close to us, and when things got really difficult, they would help each other out. But when the droughts came, there just wasn't any helping because even if you could break up the land and put the seed in, as the years went on we had less and less seed. There was nothing to leave over from the year before because we had to eat.

It sounds very difficult. Were you miserable all the time, or were you happy?

Our family was very happy. We were interested in the history of our people, so our parents made sure that we learned the dances and the songs of our people.

Did you have any form of schooling?

173

No, in the area where we were located, there weren't formal schools. Boys were just expected to grow up to be farmers or hunters and women to cook and sew and do things of that nature.

What religion were you?
We didn't have what you would call an organized religion. There was something that was sort of a native, home-grown belief system that was modified a little by some Muslim beliefs that crept down into our area. It was the way that our people celebrated life and gave homage to the Great Master for what we had and for providing us with plenty (which we didn't have).

Did you have big family gatherings from time to time?
With my uncles so close, we saw them and my cousins all the time. My father, in addition to his two brothers who lived close, had two sisters who lived quite a way away; we all got together on some occasions. My mother had four siblings, as well, and sometimes for big celebrations we would go to their village, which was a day's travel away.

Did you use camels?
No, we didn't have the money for that. Early on we had some goats for milk, but that was about it.

It just got hotter and drier?
It just got hotter and drier, and it got so that the soil became like powder, it was so dry, and the winds would come up and you had to go inside and put cloths over your face in order to be able to breathe. By this time, my mother had died. She was always in weak health, and the lack of food and the conditions just got to her. She was what you call depressed and just gave up all hope, so that left me

trying to take care of my four younger siblings, one brother and three sisters, and my father.

What happened next?
When it became clear for the second year's growing season that nothing was going to grow, my father had heard through his elder brother that there were some camps three days away where they were providing food. There were now only five of us children, including me, and so my father decided to go to the camp so that he could get food for us.

He went alone?
No, he bundled us up and took us with him. It was supposed to be a three-day trip, but it took us over five days to get there because he was carrying the youngest two and I was trying to help the other two along.

How were they doing physically?
Physically they just had no energy—as I had no energy, and Father had no energy, so it was very difficult for us to move along at all.

Did you have any water?
We had very little water. There were a few places on the way to the camp where we came upon a little water, but there was over a day where we had no water at all, and at the end of that day, my youngest sister was—we were unable to get her to hear us or anything, but she still seemed to breathe a little. When we did get her some water on the next day, she seemed to become a little more aware of things, but her eyes looked funny, sort of glazy, sort of like a muddy stream.

Were you able to get her to the camp?
We did finally get to the camp, and when we got there, there were more people than I had ever seen, and they were just shuffling along. Every time somebody walked past dust would rise up. As we went to—I guess you would say—check in, to make our presence known, there were people there who took down our names and assigned us to an area within a cloth tent, and they provided us with some blankets.

Were these your own people who were running the camp, or were they people from outside your country?
There were some of our own people, but there were two white people who had a red crescent marking on a band on their head. They seemed to be the ones who were more concerned that we get settled. Our own people looked very well fed and very tidy, very neatly dressed, and seemed to stand away from us unless we got too close, and then they would direct us to do things. It was more like they did the ordering.

Where was the food coming from?
The food, they said, was coming from the north, from...

Addis Ababa?
It came in there, but they said originally it came from places in Europe—I'm not sure exactly what Europe is, but from places in Europe, and also some from somewhere called the United States.

And was there plenty of water?
There was quite a bit of water. They brought it in huge containers that came in on trucks, and we were all allowed a little bit of water. The food that was available would sometimes be almost enough for a meal, and sometimes it

would be very scarce, depending upon what shipments they had brought in.

How was your sister?

My sister only lasted in the camp for about three days because we could not get her to eat anything. We could get a little water down her but we could not get her to eat anything. At that time they kept telling us that they had medical people coming but we never saw any. So when she died that left my father, myself, two sisters, and a brother. All of them began to get very, very tired; they couldn't play when the other people came around, and their bellies seemed to grow, and they were getting very, very thin. I was to the point where I had to rest most of the day. I couldn't move in the sun at all.

Were people helpful and friendly, or interested only in themselves?

When there was food, they were very friendly and wanting to know if you knew people they knew, and where you were from, but when there was little food, they would steal it from the weak if they got a chance. Father, because he was trying to keep alive his children who were left, would give us his food. We didn't know what he was doing at first, but we found out when he fell over one day, and when one of the helpers in the camp came, he admitted to them that he hadn't eaten in three days because he had given what little food there was to the youngest ones. He never really got his strength back after the day he fell over, so he was lying there in the corner of the shelter just like we others were.

You were the strongest at that time?

I was the strongest because for some reason I didn't seem to need as much food as the others, and I had this hope that we were going to be able to wait until the weather changed. Everybody always talked about the weather, and how it had to come back, and that we would have the monsoons again, and that dream kept me going, kept me looking for things. When we did have food at night, I would go out and see if there was any way I could get anything additional, or if there was any way I could get help for the children. Every now and then we would get some white powder that, if you added water to it, tasted just like milk, and that was very helpful to the children. But most of the time it was just like a gruel of grains that we had.

What happened next?
The periods of time when we didn't have food kept increasing, and there were many more people who came into the camp, and it was becoming more and more crowded. With the people coming into the camp, the places where you could relieve yourself became overburdened, and there was nobody to help clean them because everybody was so weak. Then people began getting sick with a high fever and a rash, and then they started jerking around and becoming crazy. Father got it first, and he lasted only about 36 hours, a day and a half after he got it. When they took him away, they then said that we were going to have to move because we couldn't stay in that tent by ourselves. There were a lot of older people around and they were afraid that we wouldn't have anybody to watch over us. So they moved us into a huge area with only children in it. People would come through occasionally to take care of us, to see if we had blankets or water, or to see if we had the fever, but there were very few of them and many, many of us.

178

Then both of my sisters got the fever. One held on for almost a week with it, going in and out of consciousness. My other sister lasted about the same time Father had. Even my strong sister, after a week just seemed to shrink in front of my eyes. Then she couldn't hold anything inside, even water, and then she died, so it was just my little brother and I who were left.

I spent most of the day, when I was able to sit up, holding him. Then he stopped talking. He had become progressively more quiet, but then he stopped talking altogether and would just stare at things. There were several times when I thought he was gone, too, but then I would see him blink an eye or something and I knew that he was there. I tried finding help; I tried getting milk when I was strong enough to walk around, and I couldn't do it.

Then I came down with the fever. It was chills—you would get so cold and then you would be burning up, and it went through cycles like that. There was one period when I must have been unconscious for over a day, because it was early morning, and then the next thing I knew, it was early morning the next day, and when I became conscious, I found that my brother was dead.

Was there anyone to help you?
I lay there for half a day before anybody came around, and then they came around and noticed that he was dead, so they took him, and they noticed I was totally unable to move or do anything, and I heard them say, "She won't be here long." At that point I didn't want to be there any longer. I didn't want to not be with my family. I didn't want to go through any more of the chills and the fever and the hunger, although at that point you don't feel the hunger. You just become used to there being nothing, and it's almost like you see your body consuming your body as you

become thinner and thinner. I just lay back and closed my eyes and said to my mother and father and my brothers and sisters that I wasn't going to try anymore—I was just going to hop on to where they were, and immediately it was like the happiest, grandest time I could ever remember. I had a sense of floating, and the temperature was just right, and there was no fever, and no aches and pains. I looked up and there was a huge light around me, and then I saw my parents and my brothers and sisters come running toward me, and I knew that I was in the land of the Great Creator.

And was there anyone else besides your parents and siblings?
Oh, there were a lot of relatives who had also been through what we had suffered, and had gone over to the Other Side.

Did you look down at your body?
I did, and I saw that they were just taking it out and putting it in a bundle with other bodies, and I felt a relief, so to speak, that I no longer had anything to do with that sense of being in charge of a solid thing. It just felt so good to be free and to be light and to be able to drift wherever I wanted to go.

Had you made a choice, before you were born, to come down to that sort of poverty?
I had made the choice that I wanted to experience the love and interaction of a big family. I wanted to experience having a lot of responsibility at a very young age to see if I could handle it. I knew that it was going to be a short life because it was going to be very, very intense. I had planned to experience all sorts of traumas and instances where people left me, and where I would go through the feeling that I hadn't done everything that I could, since I was

dealing with responsibility, and at the same time feeling a little abandoned and feeling the weight of everything. I succeeded in doing all of that. I learned so much about human emotions and what people can put up with physically when they are determined to do something— how they can push themselves and what benefits they can get out of it: the love, and being able to hold people up and help them.

What's next for you now?
Well, next for me is going to be what we call an R&R life— rest and relaxation. I'm going to plan it out so that I will use my mind in my next lifetime and have all of my bodily needs taken care of so I don't have to worry about that. I'm going to pick out a couple of parents who are going to be not extremely wealthy but in the upper level of income so that they don't worry about money. I'm going to have a fascination with music in my early years, and then I'm going to go on to some type of intellectual pursuit.

We wish you well in your next life, Ayana. Thank you for coming and telling us how you died.
Thank you for having me.

How I Died (and what I did next)

The Soldier

Tell me a little about your background, Luis.
I was a resident of the country of Colombia. My father was a bookkeeper in one of the large corporations. I was the eldest of three boys, and we had a little sister.

You lived in a city?
For a lot of my life we lived in Bogota. I went through school in the area. I was a very good football [soccer] player, and at one time had hopes of being able to play on the World Cup circuit, but I wasn't that good. I was good for a schoolboy but not good enough to take it any further than that.

Were you disappointed?
Yes, I was disappointed because it seemed to be exciting and a way to be right there in the battle, in the competition. I really enjoyed trying to beat opponents— not in a nasty way but just being able to prove that I was better. So when I saw that I wasn't going to be able to be a professional athlete, my father tried to direct me into finance. He thought that would be a good thing for me to do, but I wanted something with more action; I didn't want to be confined to an office, so I started studying politics. The idea hit my head that if I got enough experience I would be able to run for political office, and then I'd be able to make a difference for people—but I wasn't sure exactly how I was going to do that.

Then one day a gentlemen from the government came to the school and started telling us about the government's fight against the drug lords and how the political hierarchy as a whole was being infiltrated by the drug people so that they were able to take their product and undermine everything our country stood for—for the people, for liberty and democracy.

So you were getting excited at the thought of making a personal contribution.
Not only making a personal contribution, but becoming a hero so that I could then use that to springboard myself into a political career. So it was through these gentlemen that several of us found ourselves transferred to a corps of officer trainees.

At a military school?
Yes, but it was and it wasn't a military school because for part of the time we went to the regular university and for part we had courses just by ourselves, given by military people. It was almost a clandestine operation, which was also very exciting. At this time I was just 20 years old, and I could see that I was going to be able to make a difference.

Did they put you in a uniform?
Not initially, not until we finished our schooling. They wanted to make sure that we got our degree from the university because we were going to be officers, and there is a lot of prestige within the military if you have a degree. So we continued with our degrees in political science, politics, government, things of that nature, so that we could work within the structure of what we were hoping to change—to produce a whole new hierarchy within the government.

Were they paying you students?

Yes, they were. They were taking care of all of our university expenses as well as housing and a little stipend. So much of it was secret. I wasn't able to tell my father everything I was doing, only that I was involved in a project with the government, which he was not too happy about because he thought it was just some other way I had found to play. He always considered my football to be playing.

How did your mother react?

At first my mother was proud, but then when she thought about it, she sensed what I was getting myself into, because she knew that the government's main thrust was to wrest back control of the country from the drug lords, and she feared instinctively that I was going to be thrown into the lion's den.

So what happened next?

Once we graduated from the university, we went off to join the military officially. We joined as officers and went to a type of boot camp. This boot camp, instead of being only about the ideology and the principles we had studied in university, got us into using the tools of the trade, which were guns and explosives—everything that we needed in order to go to war.

There's real war on with the drug lords.

There is a terrific war going on—it is constant. There are spies on each side who are infiltrating the other. The drug lords are infiltrating the government and the military to find out what the plans are. The military are trying to employ the local people who are doing the farming and processing of the drugs to try to get them to provide

185

information for us so that we know where to go and strike: where the production plants are, where the major farming is taking place, and where the leaders of the organization are located.

It's a very complicated situation.
It's extremely complicated because it goes across all socioeconomic boundaries. It spans the entire country. It goes into areas that are not heavily populated, where the drug lords own the property and control the people on the property through fear. It's a very difficult thing to stop. What is being produced in Colombia is being distributed throughout South America, up into Central America, and up into North America. It's a substance that's so addictive people will do anything to get it, which is increasing the crime rate. It was an honor for me to be put into a position where I could help stem that flow.

Did it then become apparent to your parents what you were doing?
As soon as I graduated officially from the military officers' school and went home in my uniform.

What was their attitude then?
There was pride, but mostly fear. They knew that the average longevity of somebody fighting the drug cartel, if it was in a front-line position, was six to nine months.

And how did you feel about that? I presume you weren't unaware of that fact.
I put it out of my mind. I felt invincible, just as I had always felt on the soccer field. I felt that so long as I was prepared in body, mind, and spirit, I did not have to worry about anything. That I would be doing so much good for my country and for the world was all that mattered to me.

What was the nature of the lesson your soul was learning?
I had several lessons that were involved in this package. One was in believing in myself, being able to have clarity on how a single person could affect a large range of people. It also had to do with learning discipline because, before I got into sports, and definitely before I got into the military, I was very undisciplined as a lad. I was always into trouble. This taught me to be able to put my entire effort toward a purpose.

Do you feel that you learned your life-lessons?
I did learn my life-lessons. The only thing I did not learn was to be totally aware of the fragility of the human body. I knew the energy that was my soul. I knew the strength of a soul, but I felt that that strength was within my body.

We're to the point where you got into trouble. Tell me about it.
Before the trouble spot, I began to lead patrols into some of the inner areas. We had what was known as a strike patrol. We would be brought in by helicopter and dropped into a particular area to go in and blow up factories that were producing drugs. We were constantly gathering information by our infiltration. If we didn't know where particular factories were located, we would go and find the village elders in these little outlying places. We would try to gain their confidence and offer them support against the drug lords who were ruling their lives, to get them to give us the intelligence we needed in order to pinpoint the factories.

Weren't the factories hidden away in the forest?
They were in the deepest of the jungles. We also began to send recruits in—local boys who had seen their families

torn apart by the drug trade—as scouts, to get jobs, either cutting the poppies or producing at some of the various stages, and then to report back to us. My work alternated between the strike force and the intelligence gathering. My particular unit was significant in taking out one whole section of drug production and control. This was over an 18-month period, so I greatly outlived the prediction my parents had of six to nine months, and I had received several promotions because of my record of success. It was also during this time that I began getting known by the drug lords.

Were you a risk taker?
Yes, but that was all part of going back to my soccer playing days, where in order to score a goal, you had to take risks. You had go against the toughest and the best in order to be able to score. I didn't know, but I was beginning to be recognized by the drug leaders, and they had put a bounty on my head. So when I went out, starting with our intelligence, they were there looking for me. I thought we were employing people to assist us, but they were gathering intelligence as to where I would be and when I would be there.

My unit was given intelligence about a particular small factory in an out-of-the-way area, actually at one end of a ranch. They told us there was very little protection around it, only two to four men with guns, because it was a small operation and it was very calm—the local people weren't rebellious.

And that was a lie?
It was a lie. It was all a setup to get my team, which had been so successful. We went in there at sunset, which had been predetermined. We wanted most of the people in the factory to have gone home so that there would be just a

few night staff and as few civilians involved as possible. The area looked exactly as we had been told it was—very minimal security. My team came in with its two helicopters, piled out of the machines, and went in to start to take over. There were outbuildings because it was a farm; then the doors swung open and there were people with machine guns and all sorts of hard ordnance, and they just cut us all down.

What happened to you at the end?
As I saw those doors swing open and I faced down a standing machine gun—it wasn't even being held; it was one that was on a platform, they were so prepared—I knew then that my number was up, that it was time for me to move on, that I had lost. At first I resisted and thought, "I'm going to plow through this as I've plowed through so many things in my life," and I just let out a war cry and charged with my gun blazing toward the machine gun. But as I felt the first rounds hit me, I knew that I was outmaneuvered and outplayed. As I had done in other games, I thought, "Well, today's not my day; it's time to resign and know that I can do it again sometime," at which point I totally disconnected from my body. As I was floating away, I saw that my men had also been killed— with the exception of one of them, who I suspect was a double agent. I left and was greeted by my grandmamma.

Where did you go?
I went into ... "the light" is the easiest way to say it. It was a place where I just floated. I felt unconditional love, I felt happiness, I felt light. There was no anxiety, no pain. There was nothing of a negative force.
When you were hit by the bullets, there was a lot of pain?

189

Yes, there was. It felt like somebody taking a huge, metal rod and ramming it right into my chest.

So death did have an agony attached to it.
It did for me because I decided to go into the fray, to commit myself totally to the fray with the possibility of maybe bettering: being able to kill the people who were trying to kill me before they killed me. It was part of my desire to always win, to be part of the game, but as soon as I realized I could not win, I released myself.

So, in the same circumstance, if you hadn't had that desire to win, you wouldn't have felt so much pain?
At the moment of facing down the barrels of that gun, I could have released.

Were you aware of that choice?
At the moment, no, not until afterward. That was part of the learning process.

So you met with your grandmother. What else did you do when you went Home?
Well, I visited my mom because I knew she would be very sad.

Was she aware of your presence?
I think so, because she had been aware of Grandma's presence when Grandma had visited her, so I'm sure she was.

What about your father?
My father went through a period when he just denied my existence because it was too painful for him. He put all of his effort into my brothers and sister.

You mean denied your loss?
Yes, he denied that I had lost. He pretended that I was still just out in the field working for the military.

Did you attend your own funeral, or wasn't there a funeral?
There was a funeral, because any time the drug cartel were successful in getting one of us officers who had been a particular thorn in their side, they made sure that everybody knew they had come out on top in the fight. So they dumped our bodies back on the local precinct.

Are you now proud of your life?
Pride is not exactly something that we feel here, because pride is a judgment—I'm better than somebody else or I'm more successful than somebody else—and that's not the way we look at things. Did I learn a lot of the lessons that I was intending to learn when I went into this lifetime? Absolutely. So if that is an indication of pride— acknowledging that I have succeeded in learning my lessons—then I guess you could say I'm proud.

What happens when you don't learn a lesson?
When you don't learn a lesson, you try to figure out why it was that you undertook it in the first place. That's the first step.

Give me an example.
Well, sometimes we have a lesson we want to experience—there are so many of them; everything is just flowing through my head right now. If we have a lesson that we want to be totally in control of things, we go down into a life and the way that we experience control is first by being out of control so that we can work ourselves back into being in control. We may start out with a life where

we get born into a family that has no money and goes from one little bit of money to get food to a side job to get food, and never seems to have what is needed. In such a lifetime, if we realize we can put an effort in and learn a skill that will allow us to get a job that will help us to have the money that will allow us to be in control of our lives, we have learned the lesson. But instead, we may get the feeling that that's the way life is intended to be, and we just let ourselves continue to go from one bad situation to another and to another. Then we are totally controlled by the environment and by those around us, and we haven't learned the lesson we wanted to learn. We learned a lot about control, but by being controlled rather than by being in control.

So when you don't learn a lesson, do you have to go back and learn it again?
We generally choose to go back and learn it again, yes.

But you don't have to.
You don't have to; everything is freedom of choice. But if you do go back, because there are so many things you know don't work, generally you choose a situation that is even more "in your face" and is a stronger example of the issue, so there is no denying in that subsequent lifetime exactly what it is that you sought to learn.

This all sounds very pressurized. Do you feel pressured to perform when you're at Home?
At Home, not at all. At Home it's just like setting up the game board, and asking if we even want to play the game.

So are you going to play the game again?
Absolutely.

Soon?

Very soon. As a matter of fact, I'm just about finished making all the contracts. I have staked out a situation in which I'm going to be a female, and I'm going to experience music, all of the aspects of music. Right now I'm thinking about having it go into dance, but I don't know how it's going to evolve.

Sounds like a plan. Luis, thank you for telling us how you died.

You're very welcome.

How I Died (and what I did next)

Abortion

(Physically graphic)

Hui Ling, please tell me something about yourself and where you lived.
I lived in a very large industrial city in southeastern China. I was a girl in a mid-level family. In other words, my father was in middle management in one of the large corporations—what we called corporations, but it was only one large factory. He always had wanted to have more power and be recognized, so, since I was very nice to look at, he decided that he would arrange a marriage for me and see if he could marry me to someone who was higher up on the social scale.

How old were you at the time?
He began looking when I was sixteen.

Did you have any brothers or sisters?
I did have one brother, and this was a bone of contention because it was during the time when the one-child rule was in effect. The way he got around having two children was that we were twins, so nobody could say anything because there was just one pregnancy.

In fact, you were close together. Was your brother younger?
By about five minutes.

You're keeping up the pretense.
Yes, he was actually closer to a year younger than me.

195

So tell me about the family home.
We lived in an apartment block where the rooms were quite nice compared to some other areas but at the same time very small. We basically had one large area, a bathroom, and a cooking area, and we would roll out mats on the floor at night.

Did your mother go out to work?
Mother took in laundry on occasion, not on a regular basis because Father thought it unseemly that he was not able to take care of the needs of the family, since he was, as he always told us, in middle management. He was actually just a supervisor at the plant.

Were you in contact with your grandparents?
My grandmother—my mother's mother—lived with us for a while. She was a very gentle soul, and nothing fazed her. No matter what happened, no matter how oppressed we got with the bodies in one room, nothing bothered her. She was the one who always brought us back to a level area. My paternal grandparents lived on a farm outside the city. We occasionally went to visit them, but my father didn't like to do that because he would say they were just people of the dirt.

So your father was a little pretentious.
More than a little; I would say extremely pretentious.

Did you go along with his pretense when he was trying to marry you off?
No, I was very unhappy with the idea because he didn't care what the person was like; all he cared about was what his position was.

Are arranged marriages normal in that part of China?

More so than people want to let on. There is always some reason behind why a wedding occurs. Very rarely is it for love. In general, but particularly with the young women, a father is trying to get a good son so he can say, even though it's his son-in-law, that he has a good son.

So tell me what happened.
When I was eighteen—it had taken my father two years to find someone—the vice president of the corporation lost his wife in an accident, and they had no children. He desperately wanted to have a son, so he went out looking, as he told the men ("the boys," as my father would say), for breeding stock. My father knew that I was a very strong person, and he sold me as a prime example of breeding stock—that I could very definitely bring a male child into the family.

How did you hear about that?
I heard about that while the preparations for the wedding were taking place. How it was presented to me initially was that Tsu Ling wanted to have a beautiful bride on his arm. Now, he was at that time more than twice my age, and not the fairest on the eye, so I wasn't too happy with this, but Mother convinced me that I had no choice in the matter. Of course, Father wouldn't even discuss it. As soon as he made the agreement, I was as good as out of the door.

Are women in that society told what to do by the men folk?
Absolutely. We had no choice as to what we wanted to do. We were given very minimal book education. We were allowed to study on our own if we wanted to, but schooling stopped at a very young age so that we could learn the fine arts of taking care of the man, whether it was cooking or

massage or anything that would take care of his physical needs.

Would that be the same for members of the [Communist] Party? Don't women have a higher status in the Party?
They do, but then, I was nowhere near that, so I never experienced it. There were several women who worked for Tsu Ling at the factory, and they were the ones who helped, along with my mother, to prepare me for the wedding. They were telling my mother what all the gossip was at the factory concerning the marriage, and that I was considered by all only to be breeding stock. My mother got extremely offended and confronted my father, who for the first time that I knew, slapped her very, very hard. After that she remained completely silent during the rest of the preparations.

The preparations were for your clothing and your dress?
Clothing, dress, instructions as to what was expected of me on the wedding night, how it was going to be different when I went with him because of the fact that he had a very large house and household. It was exciting for me in the beginning because I was going to go from my one-room living arrangement into a multi-room house, and I was very excited about that.

I'm sure you were.
I also had to find something to look forward to, because I did not really look forward to being the wife of somebody whom a lot of people considered to be very cruel and mean and whom people were unable to talk to.

And was he, in fact, like that to you?
Yes. There was no such thing as a courtship. It was just, you know, your father has given you to me. Those were his

words: "Your father has given you to me, and I am going to have you give me a son."

And how long a period of waiting was there between the decision and the actual marriage?
Normally there would have been at least a year of preparation and everything else, but he was desperate to have a child, so everything was done in two months. We went from the first announcement of my father to me to going through the ceremony in two months. The ceremony itself was very beautiful, very traditional, and we went off to a country estate that was a vacation spot for powerful people for our after-wedding...I guess you'd call it our honeymoon. During that time, I was treated with respect by the staff everywhere, and I was treated as a possession by my husband. I had no say in anything that happened—when we ate, where we ate—nor in what he did to me.

And was he not kind to you?
He was very rough. He had no compassion, no loving. He didn't care about how I felt or what was happening to me. He just looked upon me as a means to an end.

That must have been very disappointing for you.
Disappointing and frightening, because I began to realize just how powerful he was with the deference that was shown to him by all the people. When we went back to the city, I became a virtual prisoner.

In the home?
In the home. He told me that I would not have any degree of freedom to even go to the store or anything until I became pregnant, and he had a regular regimen for getting me pregnant. Every moment that he wasn't tied up at the

factory, he expected me to be ready to receive him in the bedroom.

That must have been very tiring for you.
It was tiring, and it got to a point where I just blocked out what was happening to me. I knew that the only thing that would please him was to have a male heir, and I put all of the energy that I could into conceiving so that I could get over this. I figured that once I presented him with a son, he would then allow me the freedom of not having him constantly over me.

Because he was allowed only one child anyway.
Well, he had a dispensation, because of his high place, allowing him to have two children, but we had to get the first one first. He told me that he only wanted boys, that he wanted two boys. It was almost a year of this constant pattern of his before I became aware that I was pregnant. I told him that I felt I was pregnant, at which time his whole demeanor toward me changed. I now went from being a possession that was constantly used to becoming a possession that was catered to, that was taken care of. After about four weeks, he arranged for me to see the city's best gynecologist, and I began being given very good care. He arranged also for the local herbalist to make sure that I had everything that would ensure a healthy baby.

And were the reports good?
In the beginning they were excellent, and I was then allowed to take walks in the park, in the gardens, because he decided that the child needed energy outside of the house to be strong.
But his treatment of you was only because he was treating his child.

Exactly. There was no difference in the way he felt about me. I was still just a means to an end for him. The pregnancy allowed me the freedom that I hadn't had for a year, so I rejoiced in it. It seemed I was constantly being checked by a doctor or an herbalist or somebody, and there was one female midwife at the doctor's office who befriended me. She was the first person I was able to confide in about what my union with Tsu Ling was actually like. Toward about the sixth month of pregnancy she said, "You know, we really need to find out if this is a boy or a girl."

The sixth month of pregnancy?
Yes.

Isn't that rather late?
It is late, but up until that point I was still being carefully guarded whenever I was with somebody. It was the first time that I was able to spend time with her alone as a friend, and she told me that there were several tests that could be performed to see if it were a boy or a girl. So we arranged to have the tests—and then she told me that it was a girl.

Did the gynecologist know?
No, we didn't tell the gynecologist because he was very good friends with my husband, and I knew that if he knew, my husband would then know. I talked over with my friend what I could do about this, because he had an extreme temper. I had seen him, on a number of occasions, beat the servants, and I just knew that, were I to deliver a girl to him, not only would he beat me, he would also kill the baby so that it would not count as part of his allotted children. So I talked things over with my friend and she said she knew a person who had gone to medical school

201

but had run out of money and was unable to complete the training, and who could make it look as though I had a late-term, spontaneous miscarriage.

During the time I was pregnant, my husband had been very generous with me. When I had gone out, he had given me money so that I could buy suitable clothing to show off my pregnancy. He was very happy, and every chance he got he would take me someplace and show off my large belly to people. It was a sign of his manhood that he had produced a child, whom he always referred to as his son, so I knew that I could not have this girl. When my husband was out of town for a business meeting, it meant three or four days of him not being constantly around, so I could make arrangements to have the procedure. As my friend explained, it was simply putting something inside to break some of the connections that held the fetus so that it would be expelled. I didn't know anything, so it seemed reasonable to me. This friend of hers was in a very poor section of town.

A woman?
No, it was a man, because at that time, only men were allowed to go to the medical schools, and he had been in medical school until towards the end of the training. My friend accompanied me because she knew him. We went in and it was like the kitchen behind an abandoned food-preparing area. There was a large, metal table, and he had it fixed up with a type of leg spreader so that he would be able to come in and disrupt the pregnancy. I got up on the table and he just told me to relax and began working. My friend was there. Then I felt this horrible pain.

Was there no anesthetic?
There was nothing. He said it wasn't needed because he would just disrupt the lining and the sac, put a hole in the

sac, which would cause the "spontaneous" miscarriage to occur. So he went in. He'd said there would be no pain, but I immediately felt pain, and I immediately felt wetness, which I presumed was the fluid from the sac as he had mentioned. My friend started talking to him very rapidly. I didn't know what was happening, and at that time I began having horrible contractions. It was like my whole body was fighting with itself, and there wasn't a single hair on my body that didn't hurt. Everything was sheer agony.

I heard him saying that he had to get out of there, and he left, and my friend was left there with me. Between spasms of pain I asked her what was happening, and all she could say was something went terribly wrong, something had been cut or nicked. I sat up a little bit and saw that there was blood everywhere. I began to go in and out of consciousness between the spasms. I asked her what I should do, and she said she didn't know. Then as I was in the midst of a huge, wracking spasm of pain, I lost consciousness

The next thing I knew I was looking down at my body on the table and my friend was trying to pack towels to stop the flow of the blood. My grandmother, who had passed on shortly before my wedding, came to me and put arm around me and said, "You're Home now. You don't have to put up with the degradation or the fear. It's all over." And I felt a lightness. I asked her what happened, and she said, "You bled to death. Your physical body ceased to exist."

Were you still in the room with the body?
We were above the body, looking down. Then I began laughing, and she said, "What do you find so funny?" And I said, "I find it funny that I have been able to get even with my father and my husband, all in one stroke: my father for everything that he craved and sought, and my husband for

the way he treated me, as just a possession." So I went to the family home to see what was happening, and all of the servants were sad because I had made friends with some of them. Then my husband came storming in. There was no sense of sadness or regret with him, only anger at me for betraying him. It made me realize the energy around what had been our union was nothing but what he could get out of it—which I had known but hadn't realized in those terms. Then I went to the ceremony, where my parents were, and my father and my husband got into a big fight because my husband told my father that I wasn't the strong breeding stock that he had sold him.

Sold?
He used the term "sold" and he told my father that he wanted the money back, which my father said he had already spent, so he was fired. Well, not completely, but he was fired from his job as supervisor and sent back to the assembly line.

What happened to you after that?
After that I just went with my grandmother into unconditional love and sat and talked with her and my guides (whom I remembered as soon as I saw them) and my council about all the wonderful lessons I had learned. We talked about how I had put my whole energy into my existence and was able to feel each and every one of the things that were happening to me: the betrayal, the fear, the loss of self, the total control that was thrust upon me, and I knew at that time that I would never have to repeat those lessons because I felt them completely in all their aspects.

And are you going to come back to Earth again?

I am; I don't think it is going to be too long before I return—and I am not going back to China. I am going to go to a place where political freedoms are much broader.

Will you come back as a man or a woman?
That hasn't been decided yet. That's the last thing I have to decide. I've decided what lessons I want to learn, but there are all kinds of aspects of the lessons, so I haven't decided my sex yet.

We wish you well in your new life, and thank you, Hui Ling, for telling us how you died.

How I Died (and what I did next)

Section II: Postmortem Issues

Explanation

Up to this point we have printed the accounts that twenty souls gave us about a wide variety of circumstances leading up to their latest physical death. They detailed what it felt like to die and then to transition from the heavy dimension of planet Earth to the higher dimension of Home, the energetic realm of unconditional love.

Straightforward transitions Home do not follow all deaths, however. Although the final destination for every soul is the same, the road back Home is decidedly rocky for some individuals returning from their life as a human being. In the five chapters that follow, souls give accounts of some principal variations from the straightforward story of going Home.

The first such account was given by little twin girls living on a farm in Italy. After the accidental fire which cost them their lives, they were deeply frightened at the thought of their parents' anger at what they had done. Full of fear, they stayed in hiding in the back of a barn for a very long period of Earth time, slowly venturing out in their discarnate state until it slowly dawned on their terrified minds that they were actually dead. Only when that thought occurred were they able to start on their way Home.

Being lost is a relatively common experience, especially for those souls who have not been on the "wheel of life" for many incarnations. But even quite experienced souls can be very upset or angry, unaware that they have died, or frightened as to what dread experience may follow their physical death. The legions of "ghosts" in human history and fable are the result of the dislocation of returning souls who become thoroughly stuck and are lost between Earth's third dimension and the fifth dimension of the spirit world.

Modern physics in regard to the energetic universe helps to explain the term "dimension." Our knowledge of the material world's atomic structure has led to a general agreement among scientists with Einstein's discovery that every physical thing, great or small, is composed of energetic particles, and that we humans live in a wholly energetic universe. The concept of dimensions reminds us of radio waves. At one wavelength we may hear talk radio, at the next pop songs, and at a third a symphony is being played. We read the numbers on the dial of the radio as if they were separate wavebands, although in fact one wavelength merges into the next in the way beautiful colors in the evening sky merge from orange to red seamlessly.

Dimensions represent different energetic levels in the cosmos. Planet Earth, and the rest of the material universe, exists at the wavelength of the third dimension. This is the physical world in all aspects, including humankind. The fifth and higher dimensions are the non-physical, or, more accurately, the metaphysical world.

There is an energetic interface between these two realms: the fourth dimension, which is a state of being where souls may sometimes exist, displaying the appearance of a non-material body, a replica of the one that has just expired. These "discarnate" souls may or may not be visible to human beings and animals in the third dimension. They remain unique souls, despite their appearance, and they continue to be energetically stuck in the fourth dimension until they personally make the decision to go Home. During this period, a discarnate in the fourth dimension is not within the energy of the fifth dimension, the spiritual world, although its guides are able to communicate with it from their energetic base.

When the little twins died in the fire, their fear, a heavy negative impulse, held them in the fourth-dimensional interface. They could see and communicate with each other, but could only see and not communicate with their parents, although they tried. They were in the same state as Cialia, the girl who died in the tsunami flood—able to walk through material objects but in a state of temporary suspended animation, existing between the physical world and the spiritual world.

There are many variations in this energetic situation as you will see, but this basic, rough explanation must suffice. Souls get into a variety of pickles, mostly out of fear, anger, or an inability to work out what has happened to them. Retaining aspects of their human personality, they range from being mildly bothersome to being a downright nuisance to human beings, and even a threat to human happiness. But difficult or benign, all these souls have essentially lost their way, and will remain lost until the gentle whispering of their spirit guides finally helps them to open their mind to the reality of their existence and to start the process of transition with the admission to themselves that it is time to do so.

We comment on these postmortem shenanigans because they take place with reasonable frequency. Often souls are lost because, when human beings, they have not taken enough notice of the good choices open to them. This is especially true when discarnates attach themselves to living people. Their ability to do so always depends upon the actual or implied permission given by the human being who is the object of their apparent attack. Grief, depression, alcohol or drug intoxication, partaking in black magic rituals, or playing with Ouija boards and the like, can lead to human beings' becoming open to discarnates' seemingly innocent requests to befriend or comfort them. The discarnates put their hosts at serious risk of trouble when they hop inside the human beings' body space.

Discarnates themselves may make bad choices. Here our advisors, the Masters of the Spirit World, would cite religious as well as secular misinformation, along with the negative culture of using curses and the evil eye, as causes of some people being misled and suffering in consequence from being stuck in the limbo of the fourth dimension. We all possess the ability to opt out of believing people's nonsensical ideas when they do not convince our heart.

Some discarnates are infected with negative energy and will stop at nothing to make their human victims' life miserable. Whatever the scenario, we repeat, the so-called "ghost" or "specter" is essentially a lost soul. Many are curious, some may be difficult, a few are dangerous, all can be controlled and dislodged. The incidence of truly difficult discarnates is very small indeed. Now in these interviews, at long last, we have their testimony to help us to understand them better.

Ghosts

[These are twin girls from a village in the countryside near Assisi, Italy. Maria Cecilia is called Ceci, and Maria Franco is Frankie.]

Whom shall we talk to first?
C: Well, I'm Ceci, and I'm older.
F: That's not true—she's only about 90 seconds older than I am, but she always plays the big sister.

Tell me about your life together.
C: I'm the older sister, Ceci, officially Maria Cecilia. We were born into a family where there were four older brothers. We were the first girls, and of course, we're twins. The youngest boy close to us was eight years older, so we were known as the "surprise girls." When we came along, everyone wanted to take care of us, because we were the apple of everybody's eye.

F: Yes, but you always got into the most trouble and blamed it on me.

C: Well, I just was high-spirited, Frankie, that's all. Do you want to tell the story or should I?

F: I think I should tell the story because I don't glamorize it like you do. So, we were born. Our father owned a lot of land, and on the property we did farming and also had some animals that we used for milk and various things like that.

Goats and cows? Sheep?
F: Mostly goats and cows. Daddy didn't want to have to go through the shearing of the sheep and trying to find a way to get the wool to market and everything. He just kept things that could be milked so that we could make different kinds of cheeses on the farm, as well. And the boys all helped out.

We had an older brother, Franco—as you can tell, our daddy's name was Franco—who also was known as Frankie, but I was M. Frankie, or "the sweet Frankie." Frankie was married, and he and his wife lived on the property right next to ours. He had three children but they were younger than we were. At the time of the "special event," we'll call it, Ceci and I were seven years old. Frankie and his wife had had their babies right in a row, and the oldest one was two and a half, so Mommy and Daddy were always going over to help out with them because we weren't quite old enough to babysit.

What did you like to do together?
F: We liked to run through the fields and to feed the goats in particular, because the little ones were kind of fun.

But they're smelly, aren't they?
F: Oh, you got used to it—it wasn't that bad.

C: I didn't like the smell of them. They were stinky. But we had one that was a lot of fun—he used to follow us around like a dog. We didn't have dogs. We did have cats in the barn, though, but they were just to keep the mice down and to keep them from scaring the cows. We liked to get into everything. We were explorers, and exploring everything on the farm was just like being able to explore the world. We could go into the barns and follow the animals around. We had a stream that ran through our property where the animals got their water, and when it was really hot, we could go and splash in the water. From the time we were about five years old, we were very independent. Mommy and Daddy just let us run anywhere around because we were never too far away from being seen by them or one of the boys.

How did you dress?
C: We dressed in skirts, mostly, and during the summer we went barefoot. We had puffy-sleeved blouses because we both liked puffy sleeves. Mommy got our clothes from a woman who worked for us sometimes. She was a seamstress; Mommy would buy the material and she would make up the dresses. We always dressed alike because people would turn and look, and it made us feel good when people turned and looked at us.

Were your faces very alike?
C: We were identical twins.

How did people tell you apart?
C: Except for family, most people didn't, and that was what became fun, because when we went into town, we would play tricks on people. They would address me and I'd say, "Oh, that's not me—*she's* Ceci," and it would be kind of fun. But we also liked to explore things, and by the time we were seven, we started taking things apart to see how they worked.

What sort of things?

C: We had a lot of things around the farm—even things like taking wheels off wagons. We found equipment around the place that they used to cut things down, and they had big machines and we'd crawl around those and push buttons.

Did you get into trouble often?
C: Frequently, but we were always forgiven very easily because, after all, we were the only girls in the family. And they said that as much trouble as we got into, we weren't as bad as the boys had been. They just weren't used to having trouble again because it had been so long since anybody caused trouble. All four of the boys worked on the farm, so they were around, and when we would do something and they would get upset and say, "Oh, you're letting them get away with murder," Mom or Dad would turn to them and say, "You remember the time you did so-and-so?" and that would shut everybody up and then we'd get away with it again.

Tell me about the incident.
C: The incident happened in the farmhouse. By this time our youngest brother was off at school, the next oldest brother was serving sometime in the military, and the older two had their own places—Frankie was married and Giorgio was about to be married. So we were home all alone. The servants weren't there all the time—they just helped out during the day, and this was a Sunday, so they weren't around. Mommy and Daddy had gone round to Frankie's house to see about the new baby, because the newest baby had just been born, but we didn't want to go.

Because you were not interested in babies?
C: No, because we had a plan. We had found some stuff down in the basement, in some boxes, that we didn't know was there before.

What sort of stuff?
C: We didn't know, but we knew it had to be interesting because Mommy and Daddy told us not to play there. So we suspected that maybe they were hiding some stuff for our birthday, which was coming up. We decided we were going to have to go and take a look, so we just said that we would stay around and we wouldn't leave the house. We did have some books we were supposed to be reading, so they said OK—they were only going to be gone a couple of hours, and we figured a couple of hours was plenty of time to get down and see what was in those boxes down there.

As soon as they were gone, we went down to see, and the light wouldn't work. It was burned out, and it was too high up for us to reach. We needed light downstairs, and Frankie got the idea that we could take a rolled-up paper and use it as a torch, because we had seen this movie where some men explored caves with torches, and we thought that was a really good idea. So we wound up some paper really, really tight and set it on fire, and it worked beautifully.

Then we went down the stairs—like into our cave, you know, really exploring—and we found these boxes. Frankie was holding the torch, and we decided she'd hold the torch and I'd open the boxes. Well, Daddy had piled them up quite high—way over our heads, and the newest boxes were on the top, so if our presents were there, they were in the top boxes. I brought over a stool, and I was standing on the stool, reaching up with my fingertips, trying to get the top box, and Frankie was giving me light, and I kept telling her to come closer so that I could see what was up there.

I was starting to edge the box off, and the pile of boxes began shifting, and they fell over on us. All of the boxes were full of papers—all I saw was papers. Papers were going everywhere, and as the papers flew through the air, they came in contact with our torch and started burning, and everything started burning because there were papers everywhere. We tried to bash them out with our hands and we couldn't get them out, so we decided we had to run out of the basement, and as we went to turn around, more of the boxes got knocked over, and they blocked our way because it was back in a corner. We tried scrambling over the boxes and then our clothes caught on fire, and we were screaming and nobody was coming, and there was just more fire and more fire and more fire...and then it was quiet, and we knew we had to hide from Mommy and Daddy because we were going to be in big trouble.

Was it quiet for both of you?
C: Yes, it was very quiet.

What sort of quiet?
F: It was really strange. It was like we had been on fire, we were hurting, there were flames everywhere, and then there was nothing but ashes, and we weren't hurt, and we were just able to walk around in all the destruction.

And did you see anything peculiar?
F: Just the total burned area. The fire had burned the whole basement area and had gone up and caught the floor on fire, under the kitchen, and the kitchen had burned and partially collapsed.

You said your dresses had been on fire.
F: Our dresses were perfect after...one moment we're on fire, we're in pain, we can't put the fire out, there's stuff falling on us, and the next moment everything's over, and we didn't know what happened.

Did you suspect anything?
F: The only thing we suspected was that we were in big trouble.

So what did you do?
F: We hid. There was a place behind some equipment in one barn we had found that we didn't think anybody knew about, so we went out and hid there for when Mommy and Daddy came home.

What was it like hiding there?
F: Well, we hid there, and Mommy and Daddy came home, and they didn't look for us. We didn't know why they didn't look for us. It kind of scared us that they didn't look for us, so we figured we were so bad that they were going to wait until we came and apologized before they looked for us.

What happened next?
F: Time just went on and on and it was really strange. Mommy and Daddy were really sad, and the boys were sad.

How did you know?
F: They were crying a lot.

You could hear them from where you were?
F: Well, we came out at night because we figured they couldn't see us at night, and we'd creep into the house.

You opened the door, did you?
F: Yes, we just opened the door and walked in.

C: No, wait a minute, Frankie—we didn't open the door. We just walked through the door. Don't you remember that?

F: Oh, yeah—we were able to walk through the door— that's right.

Did you suspect something was strange?
F: We knew something was strange, but we weren't sure what it was. We know that our brother in the army was home, and our other brother was home from school—I mean, everybody was there.

Did you hear them talking?
F: They were talking about "the accident," that's what they called it, and how horrible the accident was, and whenever they said how horrible something was, we just kept thinking we were going to get into more and more trouble. So whenever they would mention one of our names, we'd run and hide in the barn. This went on for a long time, and we thought the strange thing was that we were never really hungry.

Did you sleep?
F: We sort of slept, but a lot of times we just sat and played with things. One of the kittens could see us and played with us—used to bring us mice. Ugh.

Did you have any idea of what had happened to you?
F: Not for a long time, because whenever anybody came we would hide, because we were sure we were really going to get in trouble—really, really get in trouble.

After a while we tried to talk to people. We tried to tell Mommy and Daddy that we were sorry, but they couldn't hear us, and then we began to wonder if we were still alive. We could walk through doors, all this time we weren't hungry, and nobody seemed to be able to hear us, so then we started talking: maybe we were ghosts ... and that scared us, so we stopped talking about it and just went on for a while. But then it was almost like a couple of years, because there was the change of seasons, and that's a long time to be scared, so one day Ceci said, "Why don't we just see if we can pray for help?" For the longest time we hadn't thought about that. The only thing we had totally concentrated on was not being caught for what we had done. We remembered when we went to church, so we knelt down and we prayed for God and our angels to come and help us, and when we did, we heard a voice.

What sort of voice?
F: It was the sweetest feminine voice. It sounded like one of the teachers at school, the real friendly nun there. She said that we didn't need to be afraid, that it was all right, that we could come Home. That kind of confused us because we thought we were at home. She said no, that we weren't at Home, that we were at a place where we had been performing in a play. Our part in the play was to be twin sisters, and we were really part of a big, huge family.

How did you feel about that?
F: We were intrigued because we liked to find out about things. So we carried on conversations with her off and on for quite a while. Then one day we said, "We'd like some proof, because we can see what's around us, but you're telling us about another place. How can we see something at the other place?" So she said, "Take my hand and I'll show you." So we took her hand, and there was a big, huge light, and it looked like a tunnel, and there was a pathway and it was all cloudy and soft, really nice, like some of the

219

big, down comforters that we had. We started walking on it, and then Nanny appeared—our grandma—and we knew that Nanny was in heaven, so we weren't sure about that at first, but when we saw her and she held her arms out, we had to go see her. So we ran to Nanny, and Nanny told us that we had died and now we could be at peace; that we didn't have to wander the farm anymore; that nobody blamed us for what had happened; that it was just an accident; and that we had to forgive ourselves for our curiosity and come and stay with her. So we did. Now we can still see Mommy and Daddy and the boys from up here any time we want to. We can go and visit them in their dreams if we want, but there's no fear anymore, and we're back in a place of what's called unconditional love.

Thank you, Frankie and Ceci, for talking with us about how you died and what happened afterwards.

Attachment

Digger, you used to live in Adelaide, Australia.
That's where the family was living when I was born. Dad was an importer/exporter at a very big company there. And Mum, she was involved in the arts scene, painting, and working out with galleries and stuff like that.

Adelaide's a big city.
Yes it is and we were there because that's where so much of the imports and exports come in. Dad always wanted to be close to where he could go and check some of the containers when they came off of the ships.

Did you get involved in the work yourself?
I was too young while we were there. When I was four, Dad got killed in an accident on the docks. A container slipped off of one of the transfer devices and crushed him.

That must have been difficult for you.
Well, it was difficult for me because of the reaction it had on Mum. I didn't really spend all that much time with Dad before it happened, because he was always at work. But Mum was totally crushed by the whole incident (no pun intended). But she also said that she had to get out of Adelaide, that there were too many memories of Dad. We were quite well off because she was able to sell his business for a pretty penny, so we moved to Sydney.

And that's where you grew up?

That's where I grew up. And the whole time that I was growing up, Mum would go from depression to utter happiness; I guess you'd call her manic-depressive. She would swing back and forth depending upon what was going on in her life. With some of the money from the business, she opened her own art gallery because that was what she knew, and became very successful. She jumped completely into that and then, when she was home, she would want to know where I was every second of the day so that nothing would happen to me because she didn't want me leaving her like Dad did. And it came to the point where I just expected her to always be there. Once her gallery got up and running and I was in school, she would take me to school and she'd pick me up from school.

Did the other kids laugh at you for that?
Well, they tried, but I was a big boy and Mum gave me everything I wanted. And what I wanted was some, you know, jujitsu lessons. And I got those so I would just beat the crap out of anybody who made fun of me. And I really did enjoy Mum's company, because she made sure I had everything I wanted. And one of the things that she loved was the sea. So from a very early age, she saw that I started getting surfing lessons. And every chance that I got, I was in the water. And that's where I got my nickname, Digger, because I used to dig into those waves and just hold on. And they'd say that I could actually dig a wave up out of the ocean so that I could ride it.

How old were you in those days when you were called Digger?
Well, from the time I really started riding well, which was, like, about eight or nine, up until when I passed out of my physical body at eighteen.

Tell me about your passing.

It was on the water. Mum was tied up with something, and by that time I had finished my early school and didn't know what I wanted to do as far as university went or anything, so I was just taking a year off to bum around. It was the first time that Mum wasn't always at my elbow, so it gave me a little bit of freedom and I got a little bit...I guess you'd say "wilder," and a little more daring. Also at that time I was being introduced by the older surfers to drinking while they were 'boarding. We would go around to wherever the best winds were coming in Australia, because we had a lot of different locations we could go to, and I had the money so it didn't make any difference where it was. If it was close to Sydney, I just drove, because I had me a nice little Porsche with a special rack on the back for my boards. And if it was farther away, I'd fly. So I was out at the south beaches because there was this front coming in that just brought in some huge waves. We had one of those all-night kegger-barbie parties, and I was out surfing, but I shouldn't have been because my mind wasn't in it. And I got up on this humongous wave and I was going and I overbalanced and caught the edge of the board and got sucked into the turmoil right under the wave. And the board came around and hit me and knocked me out so I couldn't even swim away from the crest and the undertow and get yanked out. And all I could think at that time was where was my protector? Where was Mum? Mum was supposed to be there to make sure this didn't happen to me.

And you were in the water, drowning?

Well I guess I had already drowned because I just sort of floated off to Sydney to find her. And I found her at the gallery.

223

Were you aware that you had died?
Yes and no. I knew that I shouldn't be able to do what I was doing, but at the same time it just felt right.

So, it felt like your death came by accident?
[laughs] Well, the whole thing, I guess you could say, was by accident. You know, a very drunk person in the midst of a storm surge? I guess that's an accident.

You didn't feel anything?
I didn't feel anything at all. I was going from the exhilaration of being on this huge crest—being able to see for miles, and the next moment, as soon as I lost my balance, it was almost as if I fell off that board and fell right into Mum's gallery. That was how the timing seemed to go on it.

Did you go back to see your body or didn't you bother with it?
Well, I didn't worry about it at that time, because I found Mum and I found that I could just curl up inside of her.

Did she let you?
Oh, absolutely! I mean it was, she even patted her belly like I was, you know, back in the womb. And I hadn't been there very long at all when this officer came in and told her that her son had drowned. And she said, "I know that there was an accident, but he's safe here." So then I knew that she knew that I was there. And she made arrangements to get my body brought back to Sydney. There was a big memorial service. It was really kind of cool, because I sort of let her know what I wanted. And I mean, there was my coffin, but it was surrounded by painted surfboards. And we had the majority of the service outside. It was a really cool thing. It sort of was the type of thing that if I was going

to throw a party, that's what would be done. And at this time I was able to communicate with my Mum real well. You know, if I wanted her to do something, I would just think it and she would do it.

Do you think she was aware that you had attached yourself to her?
She wasn't at first, but I think during the memorial service she knew it. Because I was commenting on who came and what they did. You know, old girlfriends, some of my chums. After that service, when she went home, she started talking to me just as if I was in the room with her. And she seemed to be able to hear everything I was saying. And the main thing she said was she—she called me Digger—she said, "Digger, I don't want you ever to leave me. I don't want you to leave me like your dad did. So stay with me and I'll do whatever you want me to do."

And how did that make you feel?
It made me feel like I was being taken care of, that I didn't have a worry in the world, that I would never have to want for anything.

And you were aware by now that you had died because you'd been to your own funeral?
I was aware that I no longer had a body, yeah. And my choice was to stay and still be able to see the things that were there, and to be able to feel that unconditional love she had for me.
Were you able to influence what she did?
Yeah, I got her to spend more time at the ocean. You know, whenever I felt too cooped up because of all of the stuff going on at the gallery, I told her, "Mum, it's time for a long weekend at the water." And there wasn't too much

225

resistance because she'd always loved the water anyway. So I felt that I was really doing a service for her because she was getting really overworked and run down at the gallery because she was putting so much time into it.

Was she still as manic as she had been?
No, that was all gone when we were together. She knew I was there and that nothing was going to separate us.

Were you able to control her moods?
To a slight degree, but I really didn't have to do much controlling because it was like she changed. She didn't have what you would call negative moods any more because she could feel me and she knew that I was with her and nothing was going to separate us. And I knew that as long as I was there, taking care of her, giving her that energy, that she was going to be great. So I felt good about what I was doing and she was extremely happy that I was there.

Digger, there seem to be three elements in this relationship that you created by coming into her: your relationship with her body, and her conscious mind's ability to communicate with you, but also, there would be a relationship with her soul. Can you explain to us what happens when someone like you comes in and attaches to another person?
Well, I can only tell you from my experience. What I was doing for her on a physical basis was giving her the physical sensation of me being close and not going to abandon her. I was giving her the psychological unconscious and conscious effect of being able to talk to me anytime she wanted to, because we were sharing the same body. And then on a soul level, we were fulfilling this contract that we had of mother and son, and of very closely taking care of each other, impacting each other's lives—at

least that was what we had agreed to do. The real lesson for us was something different, of course. The lesson was to learn to honor our own selves and to take our own powers and be responsible just for ourselves. But our whole physical life had been so commingled that our souls, while connected to the physical, felt better commingled.

When you made the contract with her soul before coming down to planet Earth, did that contract involve in any way your being attached to her, physically?
Not really. The contract was for us to be dependent upon each other for our first physical and then emotional well-being. And it was for us to have the opportunity to learn enough about our own strengths that we could, hopefully, separate ourselves, because that was the lesson. Separate ourselves and face the emotions, the doubts, and the fears that being apart created.

So, in fact, you did not fulfill the contract?
Not during the time that I was within her body, because the whole thing was for us to decide to be individuals rather than to be a unit.

In the evaluation that you make of your life when you go Home, is it seen as a mistake to have gone as far as attaching yourself to someone else?
[laughs] No, not at all. Nothing that takes place while you are on a learning trip, which is incarnation, is considered to be wrong. It's just considered to be potentially different ways to learn the lesson that you wanted to learn. There's nothing that's right or wrong. It's just an indication of how fast you can learn something. And to some degree, people joining and infiltrating another, attaching to another, is a

lesson in itself so that you can feel not only your emotions in that lifetime, but their emotions as well.

So in a sense, you were not a lost soul. You were a soul that retained a sense of purpose?
I wasn't aware of the sense of purpose, but yes, your evaluation is correct.

How long did this go on for?
We were commingled for over three years. We began to change, or at least I began to realize that this was not helping me to move on and learn things, due to the fact that, while I was attached to her, there were day-to-day things she did that I had no interest in whatsoever. Going to the gallery, purchasing paintings, selling paintings, having shows, had always bored me when I was in physical form, and I didn't like it that much better as an attachment to her.

But you weren't able to stop it?
Well, I couldn't. As much as I could affect her, I couldn't affect her 24/7. So I could get her to take trips to the beach, I could get her to take vacations, I could get her to just spend time away from the business, but she still had to fulfill her physical needs, which were provided for by the business.

Did you have the ability, which you did not choose to use, that you could totally control her if you had wanted to?
No. She would have had to agree to allow me to totally control her, and she had always been a very strong woman, a very strong soul. So she never totally gave me control over her.

But that is a possibility?

It is a possibility, but it did not occur in our case.

In your knowledge of other people, how common is it that a soul comes in and totally controls another soul?
It's actually rare considering the number of souls you have on your planet. There may be, planet-wide, fifty- to a hundred-thousand incidences of it at any one time.

Total control?
And considering the billions and billions of people, that's very minor.

You mean total control?
Yes, total control.

How prevalent is the incidence of attachment?
Oh, attachments, if you consider from minor attachments, all the way through integrating...

As you did?
As I did: that is very frequent. There are very few souls who incarnate and don't have attachments periodically throughout their existence. It's a way for them to learn very easily about the essence of themselves, about how much power they have, about how they make decisions, their freedom of choice. So attachments are very common.

And are there souls that attach not to just one person but to a series of people?
If they are not making a total connection, yes. If they have developed during their lifetime a very strong, powerful persona, because it is the energy that they gather that they are able to spread out to people, they can influence many people at a time. One example would be motivational

speakers who, simply by being on the airwaves, can get 100,000 people to do exactly what they want them to do. The same thing can happen from a nonphysical standpoint, generally not that many people, but several dozen or a hundred or so.

But the motivational speakers do not totally control.
In some cases they like to, and in some cases they do.

Can they spread themselves thinly among so many people?
Well, they can because the media makes it easy for them to do it. If people totally accept their energy, totally accept giving their own individual power over to those speakers to make the choices that direct the recipients' lives, then, yes.

So the energy of the speaker's soul is capable of being implanted in a whole range of other people?
Yes. And there are two sides to the attachment. Like with my mother, after about three years I decided that it was time for me to move on, and that I could not learn anything more. I was being restricted because she was going more and more back to business and cutting me out more and more. At that time, I just wished to move on.

And so what did you do?
Well, I told her in no uncertain terms that I wanted to leave, that I wanted to go Home. I wanted to go join Dad. And she guilt-tripped me that I would be abandoning her, that I didn't love her—all of the psychological connections that people use to try to control other people. And I could almost feel her physically hanging onto me as I tried to withdraw.

Did you need her permission?

I did because it had been a joint agreement. It's like when you have a physical contract with somebody and it is unending: if you want to withdraw from it you have to have their agreement in order to break the bond.

So she reluctantly gave it in the end?
After about six months she finally agreed, and that was only because I did get a little pissy with her, I have to say. You know, I started causing all kinds of problems for her, making noise when she was trying to sleep, things to make her want to get rid of me. It put her in a situation where she went and sought professional psychiatric help about this voice in her head, and it came out that she, in fact, was holding on to me. The therapist convinced her that she had to let loose, and as soon as she said, "Yes, you can move on," I was out of there.

And you went straight Home?
I went straight Home.

Was your father there?
Dad was there. My guides, whom I hadn't really met or talked to much, were there. As I began to remember things, I saw old friends with whom I'd had other lives, and they were giving me a rough time about how long it took me to get things straightened out and, you know, the usual jabbing at each other.

And is it worthwhile attaching yourself to someone else?
I'm never going do it again, because in the end I learned that you don't really appreciate what you are experiencing unless you are taking responsibility for it and making decisions as to what you want to experience. And if you're

attached to somebody, you're saying that their decisions are going to be openly accepted by you as being your own.

Thank you, Digger, for telling us how you died and what happened afterwards.

Demon

Tell us your story, Miguel.
I lived in Port-au-Prince, Haiti. I was from a middle-class family. In other words, we had a fairly nice house in an area that was not blighted like a lot of my country. My family was Christian, but there always seemed to be some energy that was not lively enough within that religion for me. So when I was in upper school, I got together with a bunch of boys whose families were into what they called "the other arts." Most people would call them "the dark arts." It was a combination of religion with a bit of what you would call voodoo.

What this gave me was a sense of power and a sense of wonder, and I was able to find ways to manipulate things. There were certain spells that we would do to get even with our enemies: you know, like having them come down with an illness or get into an accident—things like that. And at the time, I had no idea what was happening. I thought it was just my intention that was doing it. But as I got deeper into it, I began to feel other energies around me. These other energies, I learned, were spirits who had left their bodies but were hanging around to help us do whatever we wanted to accomplish.

Did you have conflict in your mind between that experience and your Christian roots?
Absolutely not. I found it to be exciting, quite entertaining at times, and it answered all my questions because the ministers and the priests had always told us that this is so,

but I couldn't feel anything and I didn't see anything and had to take it on faith. Yet this was something that was palpable for me. I could feel it. I could sense those around me. I sensed the power that was building within me.

How many of you were involved?
We had a steady group of nine to twelve who got together frequently. We communicated with the energies sometimes through a Ouija board, when we would ask them questions about what we should do next: what was the best way to get even with Jerome for what he had done, or how could we help Maria to get pregnant—you know, different things like that. We would invite the spirits to enter and to come through us to answer the questions on the board. We also used a number of different objects. We had what some people call runes—we called them knuckle bones. They were knuckle bones from animals that we would throw and the combinations would give us an indication of what was the best, the most powerful thing to do. During this time I felt on top of the world. There wasn't anything I couldn't do.

Did you have secret meetings at night and that type of thing?
It started out only at night, but when I completed school and went to work, some of the people worked in the same place as I did. They actually got me the job in a chicken slaughterhouse, so it was very easy for us to do some of the rituals during the day, blood sacrifices and the things like that. One of the owners was involved with us and the others turned a blind eye because we were getting business done and everything was being accomplished. They didn't say anything about the candles that we had burning all over the place, because they did keep some of the odor down from the slaughtering. It was a perfect setup for what we were doing.

How long did this go on?

It went on for about four years and everything was going great. We began to get a clientele of people who wanted different mojo bags put together, either of good things for them or of a curse for somebody else. They wanted fortunes told, and we were able to do all that while still completing our work.

Was there money in it?

There was a lot of money in it. Once it got known what we were able to do, and how successful we had been in the past, we had a steady stream of people coming in. We were almost making more money than the company itself was taking in—definitely more than we were being paid for our labor.

How did that come to an end in your case?

Well it came to an end for me because I was getting, in my own mind, very powerful and I was throwing caution to the wind with everything I did, thinking that I was invincible. I had a couple of spirits with whom I worked who were giving me information. You would call them discarnates, or ghosts, or something like that. They were out of their body but hadn't gone Home. And they were, as one person said, "a couple of hellions." They came up with things—basically ways to get even with people, and energy curses that we could put on them, and things like that. So many people in my home town believed in it that, as soon as the word got out we had put a curse on somebody, everyone thought it was going to work, so of course it did. They were just accepting of it.

I had risen in the ranks to where I was number three in the organization, which had grown from our original nine to about fifty people. Not all of them practiced creating the curses and the good luck, but practitioners joined us. We started having large meetings on Saturday nights where the faithful came and we began inventing different rituals

And then something happened to you?
Well, what happened to me was as I got into a mindset that I was invincible, I didn't pay any attention to what was going on around me. So one day, when I was out looking for some berries in the area that we used for our mojo bags, I saw a snake and thought nothing of it until it bit me. It turned out to be poisonous. For a time I tried willing the poison out of my body, but it didn't do any good. After I had a sense of intense heat going through the body, my body began to lose sensation as it swelled up.

Were you alone at the time?
I was alone and the poison so immobilized me in such a swift period of time that I was unable to go for help. I was in a rather isolated area, and I fell down in shrubbery where nobody could see me unless they were right there on top of me. I felt each one of my body systems closing down and there was a lot of pain. During this period I thought, "I'm going to get even with whoever it was cursed me." Because by then my whole life was about curses and vengeance and I thought that somebody had cursed me and that was why the snake had been able to bite me— instead of the fact that I just wasn't paying attention. It reached a point where my body stopped hurting and went numb, and then I was out of my body. And as soon as I was out of my body I thought, "Oh boy, no restrictions! Now I can get even." So as it was a Saturday night, I went to the Saturday service in my new non-physical state.

What did your non-body feel like?
It didn't have any sensation at all.

Did you see yourself in any new way?
In my mind's eye, I was the same as I had always been.

Were you aware that you were dead?
I was aware that I was in an in-between zone. I didn't perceive it as death. I perceived it as going into the area where the helpers were. And as I went to the Saturday night gathering I saw the others, the helpers who had been present with us for years.

Were they all discarnates?
Yes, they were discarnates. We were all in that in-between state. So, they started telling me how we could influence people, that all people had to do was believe in us, or allow us in, for us to be able to enter their bodies and affect them. This was, in fact, how our curses worked: people believed they would work, so then our energy could go inside and disrupt the flow of the human body by being inside it.

You say they were all discarnates. Were there any negative energies that you could describe as demons?
[laughs] I guess you could describe us as demons because our sole purpose was negativity. Our purpose was defeating the goody-goodies. Our purpose was revenge. Everything was of a negative nature.

Where did you get your negative energy from?
Negative energy is all around. For every positive energy that somebody has, there's negativity waiting to balance it. So it's very easy to go around and gather up all that

negativity. And as people become more negative in a group, it's like putting a light on and gathering more light. You put this black energy out and it attracts all the black energy.

So tell me, how did you influence people yourself?
The very first influence I had was on a group using the Ouija board. We had basic rituals involving everybody, you know. We'd have a blood sacrifice, and all of that. Then we'd break into small groups and they'd use the bones or the Ouija board or something. I was sitting around the Ouija board where there were a couple of new people. They opened up and said, "May whatever energy is necessary for us to get our answers come into us." And I thought, "Oh boy! I can have a body!" So I zipped into this guy...

Someone you knew from the past?
No, this was somebody new, but I went into him. He started asking questions about his boss. So I started feeding him answers about things he could do to sabotage his workplace. And I was having so much fun! Then I went with him to his workplace, because he seemed a little weak. He seemed like he wouldn't go through with it. He worked on an assembly line where they built radios, and I showed him how if he put little nuts from the assembly into different parts on the conveyer belt, he could screw the whole thing up, but it would only look like they had fallen off the radios. It was so much fun, but he was really kind of boring, so I wanted to switch someplace where I could have a little bit more fun. Just as I could hop into him because he gave me permission, I could also hop out.
Were you able to be in more than one place at a time?
No, I was not.

That was because you were truly a discarnate?
That's because I was a discarnate and my main identity was still as Miguel. I wasn't a spirit as I am now. In my present form, I can be as many places as I want.

Was your physical absence noted by the group?
Well, my body was eventually found. When somebody went to gather some of the same berries, they found me. My body hadn't really been there that long because they noticed I was missing; they knew what I was going to do. So they found me in about two days. But when they found my body, I didn't care because it was much more fun not having a body.

You had a Christian burial?
Yes, my family held a Christian burial.

But you didn't go?
No, to me it was boring. It was all that lovey-dovey, goody-goody stuff and I was having much more fun playing around, causing people problems, and giving power to those who wanted it. No, I was out of that life. The only effect I could now have was on other people, and I affected those other people either by putting thoughts into their heads or by going through a series of various bodies as people said, "Let's do this, let's do that. Will you help us with this?" Because they always prayed to the energy outside of them asking that energy to help them, it was like saying, "Open the door, come on in!" And I would just hop into that body and help them cause mayhem.

You helped them by making them think in a certain way?

I made them think in a certain way, and when they were a little hesitant I got to the point where I could actually start moving their bodies in a new direction.

What was your relationship with their soul?
My soul was, of course, still within me, but I was blocking any thought of anything other than the negativity I wished to be in.

I meant the souls who were already in the bodies that you came into: what was your relationship with them?
My relationship with them was the same as a relationship would be between two people totally in body form. We acknowledged each other, but you can see different sides of a person. I chose only to see the side wanting negativity. I didn't go in and say, "Okay. You're a negative person. Let me talk to the goodness of you."

Could you have taken control over the body from them?
Well, in some places I did for a period of time. But I got bored very easily, so I would only stay in a body until I found another body that was more fun.

Did this state of affairs go on for a long period of time?
It went on for almost seven years.

And how did it come to an end?
Well, it came to the point where I started realizing that things were just repeating themselves. I wasn't having any new experiences. It was like I was on a revolving wheel that came up with the same thing over and over again. "Want to make this person fall in love with me." "Want to make that person fall out of love with the other one and in love with me." "Want to get even with him because he stole my girlfriend." "Want to find a way to get this person to

lose money." It was the same thing over and over and over again.

I started getting glimpses every now and then of bright flashes of light around me, and at first I totally ignored them because everything I was doing was in darkness. So one day, when I was between bodies and kind of bored looking for somebody who would invite me in, I went to examine one of these bright things, and poof! it was one of my guides asking me if I'd had enough, and if I wanted to join them and come into an area where there was unconditional love. I hadn't really thought about love except from a standpoint of manipulating it to do other people's wills, so I brushed off my guide at that time—but it was like a little seed planted in me.

After that, whenever I became involved in anything negative I thought, "But this negativity is possible only because people have walked away from unconditional love." The need to know what that unconditional love was like began to simmer and grow inside me. The more time I spent thinking about it, the more I had a sense that, on some level, I knew what it was. So, another day, I went out in search of one of the bright spots again and found one, but it was a different one, and it turned out to be another of my guides. We sat down and had a discussion about what I'd been doing and the guide asked me how it made me feel. I said, "Well, you know, it's fun," and everything else, and the guide said "Yes, but how does it make you feel? That is how it makes you think. How does it make you feel?" And I had to admit that I didn't really get any feelings out of it at all. I just got some quirky half-human satisfaction out of what I was doing. So he asked me if I wanted to feel again, and I said, "Well, what do you mean?" And he gave me this blast, where for a second he opened up the envelope and let me feel, and I was just totally blown away with it. He just gave me this little blast and then was gone. And I'm sitting there like I'd been run over by a huge truck!

From that moment on, all I wanted to do was be in that feeling, the feeling of being a part of something, of being totally loved and nurtured and cared for. There was no kind of nurturing in what I had been doing. There was nothing but vengeance and hate. Then I went in search of that love and as soon as the thought hit my mind, "I'm going to search for it," there I was in a huge white area. I guess you could say it looked like a tunnel because the whiteness seemed to get more intense the closer you got to it. I started walking toward it and as I did, the two guides I had talked with came out and asked if was I ready to come Home. And I said that I was ready to put my foolishness aside, and my experiences aside, to come Home.

When you came Home, what happened to you?
I met with my council who had helped me plan that former life. We had discussed that the largest portion of my life was going to be surrounded with negativity, not only in the physical but in the non-physical, non-Home aspect.

So being a negative discarnate was pre-planned?
That was totally planned, and with that I was enabled to see the power of the soul in all of its aspects: the power of the soul within a human body, the power of the soul outside of a human body, and then the power of the soul joined with the whole, or at Home. It was, you might say, the study of an infinite lifetime in the microcosm of one small life.

And all your negativity was not judged to be incorrect in any way?
Oh, absolutely not, because negativity is what we learn from while in human form, or while in that in-between

242

form. Without the negativity, we can't experience the magnificence of our true essence.

Thank you, Miguel, for telling us how you died and what happened afterwards.

How I Died (and what I did next)

Poltergeist

José, will you tell me something about your life?
I was born into a rather large family. There were seven of us children. Father was a government official, and in Mexico that meant that we were quite privileged. We lived mainly in Mexico City, but we spent all our vacation times in our summer house in Acapulco. With my brothers and me, there were four boys in the family. We were scheduled to enter into government service, as father had done. Being from a family of privilege, we boys all went to private schools. Our sisters did as well, but theirs was more a finishing school instead of one preparing them for government service.

How long ago was this?
This was in your 1950s and '60s. During that period, at the school that my brothers and I attended, we were trying to keep up with the pattern of how things were done in the United States, which seemed to be that boys acted as the jokester or prankster. And it was very big that we played pranks on each other. I was the youngest of the boys, and the middle child of seven, because it was, first, us four boys and then the three girls came after me. My brothers used to tell me that I was more girl, because I was closer to the girls than I was to them. So they used to kid me about that. One brother's friends were merciless in pulling practical jokes on me—at the behest of my brother, of course. Whenever we were in school, I would always know that

245

when I went to my locker to get my books, there was a surprise waiting for me.

How old were you at the time?
I was about 12 when the really heavy pranks started. My brother's two friends, Jorge and Guillermo in particular, were his tools of torture for me. They were the ones who would set up things. Guillermo could crack any lock, so it didn't make any difference if I changed the locks on my locker. If I got the headmaster to assign me a different locker, he was always able to get into it.

And what would he do in the locker?
Oh, he would fill it with frogs, and one time (I don't know how they did it), they actually got a beehive inside. There were lots of times when they would just take the clothes that were in the locker and tie them up in knots or soak them—anything that they considered to be a lot of fun.

Did they get into trouble for this?
It was impossible to prove that they were the ones who did it because nobody ever saw them. I knew, of course, that it was them because of the comments that they and my brother made, but I couldn't prove it. And try as I could, there was no way that I could set up a prank to get even with them. Whenever we went to the summer house in Acapulco, they were just as merciless because the three of them went together as a band. It was a big house and we could invite whomever we wanted to stay. Then they would do everything: They would take the oars from my boat. They would knot my fishing gear. They would put holes in my snorkel. They would do anything that they thought would get them a laugh.

Tell me, did you deserve any of this?

246

The only way you might consider that I deserved it was that my reaction would always be very comical to them. First I would get very mad and then, when they continued to make fun of me for getting mad, I would start crying. And that was when they would say that I was one of the girls. My life was absolutely miserable and it lasted for almost five years.

Then what happened?
Well, then what happened was we were at Acapulco. I had started scuba diving lessons. Father hadn't wanted us to scuba dive until we were 17 or 18; until then we could snorkel or we could surfboard, but he didn't want us scuba diving. I had always wanted to scuba dive so I started taking lessons. My brother wasn't interested in it, so it was one place where I got some relative peace, but I had my gear at the house and somebody put sand into the regulator. It happened when I was on a dive and it was my deep dive testing day, where I was going to go down quite deep and sit there for awhile and then go through the decompression process coming up. In the beginning, the sand in the regulator didn't work its way into the valve to jam itself until I was down to quite a depth. Then it froze up the valve and I couldn't breathe. And my last thought in my physical body was, "I'm going to get even with these guys." Because I knew immediately that it had to be one of the three of them who had done it.

Tell me what it was actually like to die.
Well, at first it was scary because I realized that I was at such a depth that I wasn't going to be able to get up in time. And somehow I had become separated from the other students in the class and was at such a distance that I couldn't get their attention. It never occurred to me, as I

247

was trying to free up my valve, to swim to them to buddy-breathe with them. That was something I thought of afterwards, but it didn't occur to me while I was going through the actual process. At first I fought it. I tried to do something about it. I tried to rise up, and was conscious of not rising too fast because they told us how horrible the death from the build-up of gases in your body would be.

How deep were you?
We were at over 200 meters—this was our really deep dive test. And as I began to go up, I was so lacking air... I had tried hard to breathe and of course I panicked, so I was trying to breathe harder, which was building up carbon dioxide. And then it was like I was in a dream state. It was as if I was moving in slow motion. And then all the panic just stopped and I realized at that time that my physical body was no longer functioning. I watched myself float up. And I actually took the time to swim around and have fun before I went and joined my body.

Judging by what you just said, you had the sense of being in a body other than your real physical body.
No, it wasn't a body, it was just a presence. It was as if you could project your mind out to some imaginary place, but it wasn't an imaginary place. My consciousness was able to do whatever I wanted it to do, to be in the physical body or to just stay there and look around and sort of float around in the water. It wasn't the perception of a body, per se. It was just a consciousness.

Did the body, itself, rise up to the surface?
The body floated up to the surface on its own.

Did you observe what happened to the body after that?

I saw the personnel on the boat take a hook and pull the body in.

And did they try to resuscitate the body?
They did. They tried to resuscitate me, but I sat laughing at their efforts. They had trouble getting the gear off my back and everything else, because the body was just dead weight at that time. One of the things I had forgotten to do was to release all of the weights. I had only released some of them. That was why I floated up so slowly. I had released some of them but not all of them. Some had gotten caught. So the men were trying to pull me out of the water with the weights and everything else. It was rather comical. But, as I said, I had decided as soon as I started having trouble breathing that for this, I was going to get even.

Take revenge?
Take revenge. I had read some stories about what they call ghosts, and possession, and things like that, so I decided that was what I going to do next.

Before we get to that, did you, in fact, follow the progress of your body to your funeral?
The funeral was held in Mexico City. Father had the body brought back to Mexico City from Acapulco. So yes, I rode along in the car with my brother and his friends, realizing that they had caused this.

And did they say anything to your father?
Of course not. They didn't dare say anything to father.

Was your death affecting them fairly deeply?

Yes, it was, at which I found a great degree of satisfaction. It was my first revenge, that they were going to start feeling those things over which they had no control, things that were in the shadows ready to pounce on them, as they had done with their practical jokes for all those many years.

At this time, before you started being a prankster, did you have any doubts whether you should be doing this?
None whatsoever. From the instant I had trouble breathing, my entire intention was to get even.

Did you not contact your spiritual guides in any way?
I heard mumblings from the side—as you would say, from the curtains on the stage—but I ignored them because I was full of purpose. My purpose was to remain a thorn in the side of all of those who had played tricks on me and ruined my teenage years.

So what did you do?
Well, at first it was simple little things. I would make sure that their homework had inkblots on it. I would take and shuffle up their homework assignments. I made sure that whatever they were eating ended up down the front of them. I would just sort of tip the juice as they were drinking it, or have the plate slip out of their hands when it was full of tomato sauce. All those little things that they used to do by tripping me and pushing me, I was able to sit there and do.

How did you do it?
I found that if I concentrated my energy sufficiently, I could create a wave of energy. And that wave of energy impacted whatever I had focused my concentration on.

Did they become aware that it was you who was doing it?
Oh, not for quite some time. They thought that they were just becoming clumsy, or that they were having a string of bad luck. It wasn't until I started escalating things that they began to think it was something outside of themselves.

Were you choosing to do this just to your one brother and his two friends, or were all your brothers involved?
My primary thrust was against the three miscreants (that was a word I picked up in school). I would do little things to my other brothers because they had laughed at a lot of what had gone on, but nothing as severe as I did to the one brother and his two friends.

So you could direct your intention to one person?
Yes. I would decide that I was going to do something such as create a huge breeze that would scatter all of their homework papers. Or that I was going to have something from a tree fall on their heads— you know, a coconut or something as they passed under. On one occasion, I even changed the stoplight when my brother was going through an intersection so that the rear end of his car got hit. He had thought he had enough time to get through the intersection, but I changed the lights so that the other traffic came streaming at him.

You were quite merciless, then?
As merciless as they had been toward me.

Were you prepared to see them die?
At that time I really didn't have a goal other than to torment them as they had tormented me. Because I was in that state between being in a body and being with the angels, I didn't know that it was a bad place to be. So if

251

something had happened to their physical bodies, so be it, just as they hadn't considered the effect of putting me in a position where I could not survive.

Would you say you were a discarnate in the fourth dimension between the spiritual and the physical?
As you classify it, yes, I was. I was in the fourth dimension because I was nonphysical. Now, as a soul, I know that people can be in the fourth dimension in their physical body as they are moving toward the fifth dimension, which is of nonphysical being. But there is an in-between place where a soul, after it has left the physical, can hold itself rather than going all the way to the nonphysical fifth dimension, the dimension of Home. That was the place I was in.

Were you not intending to go to the fifth dimension, or didn't you realize there was one at that time?
At first, I didn't realize there was one. I was so intent on creating havoc in my brother's life that I didn't concentrate, think, or spend any time on anything else.

You've said the power of your soul was directed at coconuts and traffic lights. What else did you do to escalate the mischief?
Slam doors in faces, move chairs into the way, move chairs out of the way as people were sitting down. Anything that would make them question their own sanity or their own abilities, which was a position I had been in and knew very well. When I was in physical form, I felt that I had absolutely no control over anything. I had been a puppet, a marionette, directed by those outside of me into the most ridiculous of circumstances for their pleasure. And I was doing the same for them, except I was getting more

satisfaction because I had three whom I was primarily affecting, whereas it was three onto one when I was alive.

So what did you do to escalate the mischief?
I started creating noises at night so they couldn't sleep. I started creating flashes to draw their attention to different things so that they would not see where they were walking or where they were going. This actually resulted in a broken arm for my brother on one occasion, a misstep because he was misdirected. My brother's friend Guillermo ended up in a pond one day [laughs], slipping over something, and Jorge kept walking into things. It was just amazing! It was like he was blinded and couldn't see things in front of him. That was a trick I pulled by creating a curtain in front of him. And he was always in a hurry to get some place, so by the time he realized he couldn't see what was in front of him, he'd smashed into something.

When you were doing this you were not actually touching the physical body in any way?
No, not at all. No. I was creating things around them.

Did you have the power to touch their bodies?
I've talked with other souls, and they say in order to be able to touch another body, you have to have a lot of pent-up, negative anger. I wasn't as much angry as I was disappointed, embarrassed. That was what was driving my intention. I had not allied myself with other negative spirits. To impact a physical body, it has to be a huge, massive amount of negativity generated on the Earth plane that is used against an individual. I never reached anywhere near that. Mine was...

More playful?

More playful, yes. It was, basically, in response to what had been done to me, what were considered prankster jokes. And I did not delve into any way to escalate that.

Had you made a hell for yourself?
Absolutely. I had put myself into a constantly evolving set of nonsense where after a while I wasn't accomplishing anything. I was making them miserable, but I was getting no satisfaction out of it whatsoever. And it became tedious to try to think up new things and to constantly be aware of what they were doing

But you were compelled to do that?
There was something inside of me that was compelling me, but it was also becoming so tedious to me that I started to open a little bit to listen to what was going on around me. When my focus of attention stopped being on the physical, I started picking up a little more on the nonphysical, and that's when my guides began working on me.

Were there any final tricks that you played before the work became odious to you?
Well, only one thing: I broke away from my brother's friends and kept taking my picture and putting it on my brother's bed, just so he would know. Then I found some other pictures besides the one that he had in his room and I put them in the backpack that he took to school. So I just made the message very clear to him that I was still around and I was watching him.

What happened to him? How was he behaving later?
I guess you would say he became very introspective. He thought before he did things. He was very conscious not to hurt people, not to set them up, not to allow others to pick on them. From being the bully, he became the protector.

254

And his friends?

His friends: one of them joined him and the other went on being a complete jerk who, because he no longer had the other two to rely upon, ended up getting in trouble with the police. It was around then that my brother confided in my father, I guess after seeing my picture about the tenth or eleventh time, that they were the ones who had tampered with my gear. My father told my brother that he had had a complete investigation done and that, in fact, there was sand in the regulator, but the amount they had put in would just have created some grit in my mouth for discomfort. He said that there was a defect in the gauge and that my physical demise had been brought about by that defect.

Were you present at that conversation?
Yes, I was.

How did it affect you?

It was one of those, as you say, "aha! moments," when I realized that there are things that are more important than revenge, which is a sense of trying to equal the things that have been done to you, and for you. The only important thing is how you live your life and what you do with it, not only while in the physical body, but as you are transitioning from the physical into the totally nonphysical. While I was listening to father, my two nearest guides were with me. We had a long talk after that, and I realized that everything, including my period as a poltergeist, was what I had planned to learn, to see the potential and to expand my knowledge.

So you planned in advance to be a poltergeist?

Something I never would have thought about, but yes, I did. I planned to confine myself to the Earth for some reason after I left my physical body.

And so you went Home?
Then I went Home.

How did you do that?
I cut my conscious links to the Earth, to my brother, to his friends, and to the rest of my family, and with my intention sought the unconditional love of Home and the universe.

Was anyone special there to meet you?
My grandmother was there, at first scowling and wagging her finger, but then smiling broadly and openly embracing me.

This is something that you don't have to do again, I suppose?
No, I do not intend to do it ever again.

Did you learn your life-lesson?
I learned about the way physical emotions work when it comes to taking advantage of another person, and how the action of one person has a ripple effect on many. So yes, I did learn those lessons.

When you were a poltergeist, were you aware of other poltergeists? Is there a community of poltergeists in the fourth dimension?
There can be if you join together for a particular reason, but I wasn't aware of any near me. If there is a bunch of souls who have transitioned out of bodies at one location, there may be a number of poltergeists together. In some buildings, the energy has a tendency to hold because it's extremely negative. [Discarnate] people may be there if a lot of very unhappy things have happened, particularly

around mental hospitals. There are lots of poltergeists around mental hospitals, but I didn't go to any of those places, and I didn't choose to ally myself with anybody else because this was a personal vendetta that I had against those three people.

Are poltergeists souls who always plan to be poltergeists in advance, or is it not always as planned as that?
It's generally not planned. It is generally that the soul wants to cling to the Earth for a particular reason. I was surprised when I found out later that I had planned it, or remembered that I had planned it, because it is such an unusual thing.

Thank you, José, for telling us how you died.

How I Died (and what I did next)

Hell

I'll call myself Gerard. I won't give you my last name or my nicknames so I won't be able to be identified, because there are some distant relatives still around. I was born in northern California, and my father left very shortly after I was born.

Did you have any other siblings?
Not until quite a bit later. I had a sister, but she didn't come along until I was fourteen which was about the time I left the home. My mother supported herself by prostitution, so we moved quite a bit in northern California, Oregon, and Washington State. Whenever she would become known in one area by the authorities, we would move. She primarily dealt with people in the lumber industry, who were very transient themselves but always had a lot of money, particularly on weekends. So we were fairly well taken care of. However, mother generally had to work out of whatever housing arrangement we had and she would bring the "Jacks," as she called them, into the house, and whenever they came in, I had to be quiet. When I wasn't quiet, she would beat me over the head and throw me out. So it became a pattern: whenever I heard her coming in, I left immediately.

From the time that I was five or six years old, I would have to go out. Sometimes it got very cold up in the mountainous country, and I was the last thing she thought about, so I didn't have warm clothes or anything else. I would stand outside the window, shivering, sometimes wrapped in a blanket if I'd had a chance to grab one. I'd be out there and I would wait until the noise stopped inside. I heard the door open, the car door slam, and then I could go back in. Because of this I developed both a hatred for my mother, for the way she treated me, and a hatred for men who took advantage of women, although I wasn't sure who was taking advantage of whom.

I never had much schooling because of the way my mother moved around. And she always had me slip through the cracks when it came to all the agencies, so nobody really knew about me and then they couldn't take me away from her. By the time I was fourteen, I was a very good-sized kid, and I got into a fight with one of her Jacks one night. He literally beat me within an inch of my life. My mother, instead of coming to my assistance and aid, threw me out of the house.

That must have been very tough for you.
It was tough, but what it taught me was not to care or feel about anything. So whenever I would be abused, I would go out and find an animal and take it out on the animal.

I suppose you had no friends?
No friends because I didn't exist. Mother said that if I got friends, then I would come into the awareness of the school system and the public agencies and they would take me away and put me into confinement someplace. That was what she constantly beat into my head. And since I did enjoy roaming the woods, I didn't want to be confined like an animal.

You say that she had more children after you were about 14. Did she settle down with someone?
I don't know because it was shortly around that time that I left. I was very large for my age and could easily pass for

17. I got a driver's license by doing some fast talking about birth certificates and things, and started finding odd jobs around. I know that she was pregnant when I left. I didn't ever see her again. I heard that she had had a girl from one of her customers who might have been the father—he wasn't sure. As I got a little bit of money, I lived in various flop houses and what passed for hostels along the roads in some of the larger cities.

Were you a driver?
I was a driver after a while. In some of the states you had to be 21 to get a truck-driver's license. Since I had started driving at about 15 saying I was 17, by the time I was 19 I had a commercial driver's license and then I was able to travel the interstate highways. I did the entire west coast of the United States. But I didn't like the lower part of California because I missed the mountains. The mountains were where I could conceal myself and watch and not be seen.

I have a picture of a person who was very much alone. Did you have any interest in girls?
No, because to me, the sexes were nothing more than one person abusing another, as my mother did to her clients and her clients did to her. So to me, there was no interest. To me, sex was something that was all about control. If you watched the animals in the forest, most of them copulate only to have control over the other animal. So that was how I saw it.

The first time that I really felt alive was when I was driving along and I saw a prostitute at a truck stop. She solicited me for business and I asked her was she staying there or going on, and she said well, she really wanted to go up the road. So I said, well, I'd give her a ride and we'd find a place along the way. My intention, really, was to totally dominate her. So we got up the road a bit and there was a real nice overlook that I knew about, so I pulled the truck off. It wasn't unusual for trucks to be there because a lot of truckers use that as a rest stop if they have driven too many hours. And it was not unusual for a truck to be there for four to eight hours. So we got there and I had sex with her. I told her that I was into bondage, so I tied her hands and gagged her, supposedly as part of the sex act. But after I had my way with her, then I just put my hands around her throat and watched the life go out of her eyes as she struggled under me. And for the first time, I felt truly in control of things.

What did you do with the body?
Conveniently enough, there was a drop-off right by the parking. We had gotten there late evening. I waited till there wasn't any sounds or any noise. There were two other trucks parked there. And I took and threw her over the cliff. For the next three days, I was just floating with the energy of what I had done. I felt for the first time that Gerard was in charge of the world—that I was in control. About that time I started using the French pronunciation of my name so that I thought I had an allure that the women might like.

About six months later, I had the urge again to snuff something out. Everything had been going wrong. I hadn't been making as much money because the trips weren't as good. I was an independent trucker so I felt that I needed to be in control again. It's very easy to pick up prostitutes at truck stops. They hop from one to another to another to another. And mostly, they do their business in the sleeping lofts of the trucks. It's almost like having your own motel room driving along with you. So, the first one was in Oregon. The second one was in northern California. Then there was another one in California, and after that one in Washington state.

Would you dispose of all the bodies fairly easily?
Fairly easily because it's such a hilly country. In a couple of cases I had to leave the bodies in the loft area of the truck until I could get off to a place that I could easily dump them. I don't know over the years how many I did, but it was between seven and ten, until I got caught.

Tell me about your getting caught.
Well, it was a stupid thing. I got very careless, so to speak. I started to drop a body in a place where there were too many other truckers. As I was carrying the body to the edge, somebody who had gotten out of his truck to relieve himself saw me and he thought that I was dumping a live person over the edge, so he overpowered me to save the damsel in distress. And then he called the police, and one thing happened after another, and I found myself on death row.

What was that like?
Boring. You know, during the trial and everything else, psychiatrists would come in and decide that I was a psychotic personality, that I had no feelings whatsoever and knew what was right and wrong but just didn't care, and that I was a sociopath, which was, I guess, a pretty good description of me.

All this time, I was also getting preached to by the "gossip" people—you know, by the gospel people—how I was going to go to hell and how I was going to burn for all eternity for everything I did. All of the families of these prostitutes came out of the woodwork to tell me how, you know, I was going to be damned and all, so I began to envision what it was going to be like. And it started out being like my childhood. But then it started taking on different characteristics: of fire that burned but didn't burn you, and all kinds of just horrible, horrible things. So by the time I got to the point of them giving me the needle, I was sure that I was going to hell.

Were any of the preachers trying to convert you to believing in Christianity?
Not really. There wasn't anybody who really liked me. And I think it had a lot to do with the fact that I wasn't very pleasant to any of them when they came in. So it turned out that everybody was condemning me. The night that I was to end my existence, they put the needle in and I awoke in complete darkness, and I knew that I was on my way to hell. I didn't want to move, but then I felt myself being drawn forward, so I gave in to this pressure that was pulling me.

Were you aware that you were outside of your body?
I don't know if I made the connection of being outside of my body. I knew I wasn't in the prison. I knew that I was no longer in that physical body, but I didn't know if I was a body. I could see something that was like a body because I envisioned that I would have a body when I went to hell.

Yes, go on.
And then I began to feel the heat. And I began to hear the shrieks of people in torment.

That you'd been taught to expect?
Which was what I had accepted would be the norm for somebody like me.

But you didn't see them? You just felt and heard them?

I just felt and heard things. There then began to be vibrations like fire. When I was a truck driver, you could see the heat rise off the pavement during the day, you know, in vapors. And I saw that, but I saw it in red, all round me. And I was consumed by this intense heat that was constantly there, eating away at everything. It was clogging my mind so that I couldn't think, and I felt at that time it was what I deserved for what I had been.

Were you aware of the passage of time?
Not really, because everything was the same. I mean, there were the shrieks, there was the torment, there was the unendingness of it. There was the inability to think, the inability to be comfortable, the inability to even give another person difficulty as I had done all my life. There was a solitariness that was worse than anything else.

But without a body, you couldn't feel pain? Or did you imagine pain?
I imagined pain. I imagined myself being burned, being scalded. I imagined my head being eaten up from the inside out by all these horrible screams, and it got to the point where I began screaming because of the misery I was feeling. And underlying all of it was this thought: "This is what you have earned for yourself." Just as my mother used to beat me if I didn't get out of the house fast enough, this was what I deserved for not being attentive to what was going on; this was what I deserved for having taken the lives of so many people.

How did that come to an end?
For the longest time I was shutting out as much as I could, so that I didn't have to listen to it, didn't have to feel it. And then one day it was almost as if I got tired of putting in all of the effort to shut it out. And I said, "Fine. I know this is

supposed to be eternal, but maybe if I just open myself to it, it will consume me and that will be the end." So I relaxed as much as I could. And, of course, the pain seemed to become more intense, the screaming more piercing, but inside the screaming was a little voice that said, "Are you ready now to accept yourself?" I had no idea what it meant so I shut everything down again. And then some period of time later, I opened up again and there was an even sweeter voice that said, "This isn't who you really are."

At this time something began deep inside of me, almost a recognition. I didn't know who it was, but I decided I would listen. And then there was a whole group of them who began to tell me that I was creating this hell that I was in. Being a soul (which was what made me eternal), was what allowed me to exist after leaving my human body. They insisted that I was eternal, and that as an eternal soul, I could create what I wanted. Of course, I didn't believe it, you know. It was just some other do-gooder trying to help me.

Then the sweet voice came back again and it said, "Just try to turn down the heat a little. You can do it." So I thought, "Hey, let's give it a shot, because being in 120-degree heat all the time just isn't my thing. I'm a mountain boy." So I said, "Okay, heat down," and it got cooler. Then a voice came and said, "Shut out the other shrieks. Shut out the other tormented souls." That was a little harder, but I gradually was able to, and I think it was by going inside of myself that I was able to shut out the shrieks. And then slowly, slowly, everything that I had thought I deserved—the fires, the shrieks, the misery, the pain—was gone.

What was left?
Darkness. Darkness was what was left, and I was alone, and I didn't hear the voices for awhile. And so I said to them, "Ok, I certainly don't want this darkness." And they

said, "Well then, change it. Change it to what you want."
And I said, "Well, I want to have... I want to be in the
mountains. I want to be in the fresh air." And I was
immediately on my favorite mountaintop. And I said, "Well
does this mean that I'm alive again?" And they said, "No.
This means your soul can create for itself what it feels it
deserves." And I said, "But I was such a horrible person!"
And they said, "Yes, in that lifetime, by the standards of
society, you were a horrible person. But you chose to
experience that. It was just a part in a play that you
assigned yourself. That is not who you are." And I said,
"What? What do you mean?" And they said, "You are like
us. You are part of the Creator. You are part of the Source
of everything. We are your friends." I said, "I don't have
any friends." They said, "We are your soul friends. You
didn't have any physical friends in that lifetime. That was
one of the characteristics of the role that you had in that
play."

Did it take you long to believe in what they were saying?
Well, there is no time at Home. But if you were to put it
against Earth time, it was several years of very slowly
remembering, of being able to peel off all the layers, the
insulation I had placed around myself during my role
playing as Gerard so that I could get down to the essence of
who I was.

So you began to realize that you were a soul?
I began to accept it because I could feel it—that I was a
soul, that I was the same as they. We had one tremendous
party when I finally came Home. It was like the reborn
individual shucking all of the shackles, all of the layers that
had hidden his true essence. And I am now, as they, totally
aware of myself. I have now understood the lessons I
learned as Gerard.

267

Was the Gerard experience like other past lives you have had?
No, it was nothing like anything else I had done. This was one of those times when, as a soul, I had decided to do something so contrary to anything else I had done that it was like an extreme immersion into evil. I had never come anywhere near that.

What else had you been in the past?
Ordinary people. I had been an accountant, a lawyer, a mother, a sister, even a nun in one lifetime. I had been a diplomat, a sailor, a fighter pilot. I had been a lot of different things, all dealing with issues of love, relationships, betrayal, but compared to Gerard, only minor examples of human emotions.

Why would you want to pick a life like Gerard?
I had become fascinated in one of my lifetimes with a sociopath, a person who couldn't feel anything, and I wondered what it would be like having an existence in which you were the center of the universe and you didn't really care about anything else that was there. You didn't care about your actions.

But choosing to be a sociopath means that you're going to hurt a lot of people. Why would you want to do that?
For the experience of doing that, just as my "'victims," with whom I had contracts to let them experience being murdered, wanted that experience. We don't exist in a vacuum. Every action that occurs while on Earth is an agreement between ourselves as an actor and the person with whom we interact.

What are you planning to do in your next life?

I haven't completely decided, but I did sort of like country singers the last time—something I developed while on the road. I used to love to listen to country singers. So, I think I might come back and be a country singer.

Man or woman?
Don't know. Haven't been a woman in a while so I might come down as one. I mean, somebody like Dolly Parton would really be a fun life.

Gerard, thank you for telling us how you died and what happened afterwards.

How I Died (and what I did next)

Commentary by
The Masters of the Spirit World

The Masters, who initiated and facilitated the writing of this book, are a large group of senior guides on the Other Side. They have provided us with their concluding commentary.

Death is not simply death—it is a transition

Transition referred to here is the period when individuals become aware that they are about to end that particular physical life. It encompasses their thoughts at the time of transition—physical death, and what happens to them immediately after they leave their body.

We are sure that many people are going to ask questions arising from the experiences related in this book. Some will ask why so many different things happened to these folks at the time of their death: isn't death just death? Death, in the physiological sense, is the cessation of the living organism that has been seen by everyone as, say, Jane Doe. But death is also the freeing of the soul—which had enabled the physical body to function—to return Home to its energetic environment. What complicates this simple act is that the consciousness of the soul, restricted at first by the physical body, experiences the shock of realizing it is still alive after the

271

body has died, before finally making the necessary adjustment to the wisdom of its spiritual self.

When a soul is living a human life, it has a physical and emotional consciousness of the things that exist on the planet. Earth is a place of duality. Nowhere else in the universe does a place exist that has negativity diametrically opposed to every bit of positivity. The body's responses to this duality are generally automatic emotional sensations. Past circumstances create triggers within the physical to issues of control, physical love, revenge, hatred—beliefs of all types which emerge unbidden at the time of death if they have not been dealt with previously.

As the mind approaches the point of death many switches are thrown by these buried triggers, and the ego panics. Questions run through the consciousness: What did society and religion say was going to happen at this time? What am I supposed to do right now? How much will it hurt to die? Have I done everything that I was instructed to do so that I will be rewarded on the Other Side? Will I be punished for what I did during this life? What is the Other Side like? Or, rarely, from those who have spent time working on their spiritual understanding of the life process: "Wait a minute, erase those belief systems; I control my reality!" The soul needs to release the physical connection to thinking and belief systems, and get comfortable merging into the sensation of the universal energy.

All souls incarnate to experience physicality and learn from daily life events here on planet Earth. They freely choose their lessons before coming to Earth. The purpose of their life is to go through the lessons and to remember their essential nature. They cannot remember who they truly are until they have cleared away the lessons they planned. Awareness of these lessons comes to them through fears and doubts. If they spend time trying to find the cause of their fears, they will find the lesson they seek. If they examine their doubts, they will find the personality issues they have set up. This gives them an opportunity to complete the lessons. But all this will still be in the way of an easy transition if they did not finish the lesson and have not cleared away the accompanying emotions.

We are sure that some of you are asking: is the death scene itself something that was planned by the soul? The answer is: sometimes. The timing of the death may have been part of an arrangement with other souls to help with their lessons. Possibly the soul has finished its own lessons and leaving the Earth will allow a partner, relative, or friend to see a hidden lesson which comes to light with the soul's passing. The manner of death may itself be part of a lesson: addiction, inattentiveness to the present, deprivation, violence, neglect, are all life-lessons. If you don't get it this time you know what you will have to work on in your next life.

And what of the after-death situation? As you see in this book, some souls fought to stay connected to the physical. This was caused by strong emotions which they chose to continue feeling. These souls remained between the physical and non-physical because they would not let go. Others created unpleasant scenarios, believing it was what they deserved. They remained there until they overcame the last fears and doubts separating the soul in its physical form from the non-physical soul which is a part of Source. Then their transition could be completed.

Once souls released the physical and accepted their nature as part of the universal Source, they were able to embrace unconditional love and join their soul mates and friends. Some did it on their own, but many were assisted through the process by their own council of advisors, other guides, and soul mates. Once comfortable again in this magnificent energetic environment, they reviewed the just-terminated life to ensure they had attained an understanding of the lessons they had experienced. Then they were Home.

An Earth writer once said: "Death is the great equalizer." If only he had known how true his sentiment is. Physical death allows the soul to reunite with the Source energy in the universe where all souls are equal—they just have different stories to tell about their lives.

In every phase of your existence, follow the rule of love, light, and laughter. We are all composed of unconditional love. We are all one in the magnificence of the light that is without darkness and negativity. And laughter helps us understand and endure, while in physical form, the things we ask of our self in the name of learning. We honor your journey, as we ask you always to honor yourself.

The Masters of the Spirit World

The Authors

Toni Ann Winninger, JD, CH, is a Reiki master and metaphysical hypnotist. She has a flourishing international practice as a psychic channeler, and teaches shamanistic Light Language. A native of Chicago, Illinois, her working life included twenty-seven years as a prosecutor for the busy Cook County State's Attorney's Office in Chicago, before being called by the Masters to be a channeler. Toni's task in this book was to channel accurately the thoughts and words of 25 souls who were interviewed by Peter.

Peter Watson Jenkins, MA, MH, is a clinical master hypnotist, working in the metaphysical fields of past-life and inter-life regression, and energy release, and EFT. A Cambridge University (UK) graduate in theology, he was a parish minister, and is the author of: *Escape to Danger* (2001), *Training for the Marathon of Life* (2005), *Christy's Journey (*2008), *Disarming Death* (in publication), *Fine Writing* (in publication), and books listed below.

Celestial Voices, Inc.

We hope you found this book a challenge and inspiration. We are the human "voice" of the Masters of the Spirit World, working to promote their messages. We have three websites for your further enrichment. Two promote the messages from the Masters and public discussion on the Masters' blog: **ReincarnationGuide.com** and **Facebook/ Reincarnation Guide.** On these sites we publish the Masters' regular messages and provide a place for your comments on a variety of topics which are chosen from the questions that people have asked them. Informative and interesting! Celestial Voices' publications are detailed on the two websites and on **CelestialVoicesInc.com**. Books are also available from Amazon.com   and ebooks from Amazon Kindle, Kobo, Nook, and Sony Reader.

Details of publications
The Masters' Reincarnation Handbook: Journey of the Soul
The Masters' systematic analysis of the process of reincarnation (2009). a brief, definitive essay.

Healing with the Universe, Meditation, and Prayer (2007)
The Masters please many readers by their cool appraisal of society's current medical scene. and of healing methods.

Dialogues with Masters of the Spirit World

I. *Talking with Leaders of the Past* (2008)
The Masters' discussion of reincarnation is followed by dialogues with the souls of 15 prominent people born in the nineteenth century: *Andrew Carnegie, Winston S. Churchill, Charles Darwin, Albert Einstein, Mahatma Gandhi, Adolf Hitler, William James, Pope John XXIII, Carl Jung, Dwight Moody, Florence Nightingale, Eleanor Roosevelt, Bertrand Russell, Margaret Sanger, and Oscar Wilde.*

II. *Talking with Twentieth-Century Women* (2008)
Dialogues with the souls of 21 prominent women from Mother Teresa to Marilyn Monroe.

III. *Talking with Twentieth-Century Men* (2008)
Dialogues with the souls of 21 prominent men from Martin Luther King Jr to John Lennon.

Breinigsville, PA USA
14 March 2011
257600BV00003B/72/P